For Reference

Not to be taken from this room

AMERICAN CITIES CHRONOLOGY SERIES

MIAMI
A CHRONOLOGICAL & DOCUMENTARY HISTORY

1513-1977

Compiled and Edited by
JAMES E. BUCHANAN

Series Editor
HOWARD B. FURER

1978
OCEANA PUBLICATIONS, INC.
Dobbs Ferry, New York

To the memory of Sylvia

Library of Congress Cataloging in Publication Data

Main entry under title:

Miami: A Chronological & Documentary History, 1513-1977

   (American cities chronology series)
   SUMMARY: A chronology of important events in Miami's history accompanied by pertinent documents.
   1. Miami, Fla.—History—Sources. 2. Miami, Fla.—History—Chronology. [1. Miami, Fla.—History]
I. Buchanan, James E.
F319.M6M62   975.9'381   77-27462
ISBN 0-379-00616-2

©Copyright 1978 by Oceana Publications, Inc.

All rights reserved. No part of this publication may be reproduced or transmitted in any form or by any means, electronic or mechanical, including photocopy, recording, xerography, or any information storage and retrieval system, without permission in writing from the publisher.

Manufactured in the United States of America

TABLE OF CONTENTS

EDITOR'S FOREWORD iv

CHRONOLOGY
    Colonial and Pioneer Origins, 1513-1895 1
    An Emerging Resort Center, 1896-1922 5
    Boom Time in Miami, 1923-1926 17
    Depression, War, and Progress, 1927-1956 26
    Miami Under Metro, 1957-1970 46

DOCUMENTS
    A Spaniard Marooned in Dade County, 1575 66
    Expansion Brings Incorporation, 1896 70
    Politics and Merrymaking, 1907 72
    The Commission-Manager Plan for Miami, 1921 75
    The Bankers' Ticket, 1921 78
    Boom Time in Miami, 1925 81
    Selling Paradise, 1925 84
    Syndicates for Speculators, 1925 87
    The Binder Boys, 1925 90
    Destruction Rakes Miami, 1926 93
    Assurance from the Mayor, 1926 96
    Humanitarian vs. Economic Interests, 1926 99
    The Assassin's Bullet, 1933 102
    A New Solution to Mounting Metropolitan
        Problems, 1954 104
    Metropolitan Miami-Dade County's Home
        Rule Charter, 1957 111
    Metro and the Challenge of Localism, 1958 119
    Diversifying Miami's Economy, 1965 121
    Chief Headley Gets Tough, 1968 125
    Liberty City Rocked by Riots, 1968 130
    Cubans Prosper in Miami, 1969 136
    Social Scientists and the Police, 1970 140

BIBLIOGRAPHY 143
    Primary Sources 143
        Official Publications 143
    Secondary Sources 144
        Books 144
        Memoirs and Accounts by Contemporaries 145
        Articles 147

NAME INDEX 153

EDITOR'S FOREWORD

This slim volume is intended as an introduction for students interested in the history of Miami. Its chronology, documents, and bibliography do not present a definitive history of the city. The information presented here is, rather, a broad skeletal view of its development; allowing the reader to pinpoint areas of particular interest and suggesting the variety of sources available to researchers.

The chronology has been compiled largely from published sources and newspapers, the object of which is to provide a chronologically and topically balanced view of Miami's evolution. The documents flesh out the skeleton a bit, mixing selections from dry but essential municipal documents with pieces on various aspects of the city's history.

The degree to which this volume aids and encourages further research on Miami's development will be the measure of its success.

James E. Buchanan
Alexandria, Virginia

CHRONOLOGY

COLONIAL AND PIONEER ORIGINS

1513   March 28. An expedition commanded by Spanish explorer Juan Ponce de Leon sighted the Florida coast.

1545   Hernando d'Escalante Fontaneda became the first recorded white man to traverse Dade County after surviving a ship wreck on the Florida Keys. He spent 17 years in Florida as an Indian captive.

1567   Pedro Menendez de Aviles, the Spanish Governor of Florida, established a Jesuit mission and a fort at Tequesta, south of the mouth of the Miami River.

1568   April. Spanish soldiers abandoned Fort Tequesta under threat of attack after they had killed the uncle of a local Indian chief.

     November. Spanish friendship with the Indians was reestablished and the Jesuits erected another mission. Its fate is unknown.

1743   Jesuits established the San Ignacio mission at what became Coconut Grove. They sought religious conversions, while Spanish soldiers tried to secure the coast against English freebooters who preyed on Spanish shipping.

1763   Spaniards transported the last of Dade County's Calusa Indians to safety in Cuba. They were being pushed by the southward moving Creeks.

1796   The first land grant in Dade County was issued to Frank Lewis by the King of Spain.

1808   February 27. The Spanish crown granted John Egan 100 acres situated where Miami now stands. This parcel of land ultimately passed into the hands of Julia D. Tuttle.

1819   February 22. The United States purchased Florida from Spain.

1825   The territorial census placed South Florida's (below the Suwannee River) population at 317.

1826   The first Cape Florida lighthouse was built.

1830   The first federal census cited South Florida's

population as 517.

1834	Fort Dallas was established as a naval base at the mouth of the Miami River. For two years, the Navy patrolled Biscayne Bay and scouted the adjacent land area.
1835	The first Post Office in Dade County was established on Indian Key.
1836	July 23. Indians burned the Cape Florida lighthouse, killing a black worker, Aaron Carter. Dade County was officially established by an act of the territorial legislature.
1839	January. The army took over Fort Dallas which still consisted of temporary buildings. December 25. Dr. Henry Perrine arrived at Indian Key to begin his experiments in tropical agriculture on land granted for that purpose by Congress.
1840	August 7. Dr. Perrine and 6 others were massacred in an Indian raid on Indian Key led by Chekika. December 4. Ninety men in 16 canoes left Fort Dallas and proceeded to the island hideout of Chekika's band. In a surprise attack, Chekika was killed. Dade County's population was 446.
1844	Miami replaced Indian Key as the county seat of Dade County.
1845	Dade County's first manufacturing establishment emerged when Thomas and George Ferguson built a mill on the Miami River to extract starch from coontie roots.
1849	William F. English from Columbia, South Carolina began construction of a permanent stone residence and slave quarters on the site of old Fort Dallas.
1850	Dade County's population was 159. A post office was established at Fort Dallas with George Ferguson as postmaster.

	By now, all English plantations in the Miami area had been abandoned because of the threat of Indian attacks and general lawlessness in the region.
	Land on the north bank of the Miami River was in the possession of the Biscayne Bay Company, a Georgia organization.
1855	The Army reoccupied Fort Dallas, taking advantage of the buildings constructed by William F. English.
1858	June 10. Fort Dallas was abandoned by the Army after soldiers located and cut off the Seminole's last supply route.
1860	Dade County's population was 83.
1861-65	During the Civil War, Fort Dallas became the refuge of a disparate collection of Confederate and Union deserters, Union spies, and blockade runners.
1865	Edmund D. Beasley received the site of nearly all of present-day Coconut Grove as a grant for his services in the Civil War.
1870	Dade County, with an area considerably larger than now, boasted a population of 85.
	Mail service was established between Miami and Key West.
	William Brickell purchased 640 acres on the south side of the Miami River and opened a trading post at Brickell Point.
	E. T. Sturtevant, the father of Julia Tuttle, bought a 160-acre homestead north of the river.
1873	Coconut Grove's Post Office was opened.
	Julia Tuttle arrived in the Miami area for the first time and bought 640 acres of land north of the Miami River.
1875	Dade County revenues amounted to $285.00.
1880	Dade County's population was 257.
1881	The State Superintendent of Schools assigned

a teacher to the Biscayne Bay region of Dade County. He traveled from place to place, teaching children in their homes.

1884   The Peacock Inn, Dade County's first hotel, was opened in Coconut Grove by Jack Peacock.

1886   The first organized school in the Biscayne Bay region opened at Coconut Grove with 10 pupils in a log cabin.

1887   The first Circuit Court in Dade County convened in an old Fort Dallas barracks, with S. K. Forster as presiding Judge.

The Biscayne Yacht Club was organized under the leadership of Coconut Grove's leading citizen, Commodore Ralph Middleton.

1888   In a county election, Juno won the county seat from Miami.

1890   Dade County's population was 861.

1891   November 14. Julia Tuttle took up residence in Miami.

Julia Tuttle offered James E. Ingraham, president of the South Florida Railroad (Sanford to Tampa) enough of her Miami land for a town site, if he would extend his railroad to Miami. Ingraham refused the offer.

Flora McFarlane founded the Coconut Grove Housekeeper's Club, Florida's first federated women's club.

1892   Standard Oil millionaire Henry M. Flagler obtained a charter to extend his Florida East Coast Railroad to Miami, but displayed no hurry to begin work.

1894   The first of the "Big Freezes" struck northern and central Florida doing severe damage to citrus crops. This aroused the interest of Henry Flagler and others in Miami as a potential citrus-growing region.

1895   Following the "Big Freezes", Henry Flagler visited the Miami area. He was offered extensive lands by Julia Tuttle (north of the river) and William Brickell (south of the river) if he would agree to extend his railroad to Miami, and install waterworks and other civic improvements. Flagler accepted and signed a contract with Julia Tuttle.

In the St. Augustine offices of Flagler's railroad, A. L. Knowlton laid out Miami's original townsite.

Julia Tuttle and her son began construction of the Miami Hotel to house workmen flooding in as the railroad approached. They also built a number of stores for renting to early merchants.

Dade County's population was 3,322.

Sometime during the winter of 1895-96, Miami's first public school was opened, attended by approximately 20 pupils.

AN EMERGING RESORT CENTER

1896

March 3. With the Florida East Coast Railroad now as far south as Fort Lauderdale, Flagler sent workmen on to "start the city" at Miami.

March 15. Ground was broken for Flagler's luxury Royal Palm Hotel.

March 26. Brothers John and E. G. Sewell opened their shoe store, the first store north of the Miami River (where the city's business district would eventually be located).

April 15. The first passenger train entered Miami on the Florida East Coast Railroad.

May. Miami's population now stood at about 1,000, with many settled in shacks and tents.

May 2. Miami's first bank, the Bank of Bay Biscayne, was established by William Mack Brown.

May 15. Miami's first newspaper, the *Miami Metropolis*, published its first issue.

May 21. Henry Flagler inaugurated regular steamship service between Miami and Key West with the steamship *City of Key West*.

July 28. With a population of about 1,500, an incorporation meeting was held. Acting under the state's general law of municipal incorporation, voters approved incorporation, selected the name Miami (replacing Fort Dallas), chose John Reilly as mayor, and elected seven aldermen.

October. Miami's first street grading was undertaken.

December 25. At 4:00 A.M. a fire broke out in Brady's grocery store. Miami was caught without fire fighting equipment, and three blocks of the business district were destroyed. One life was lost in an explosion.

December 31. By now, Miami boasted fifty business establishments, along with lawyers, doctors, and real estate agents. Flagler had also installed the initial water and light systems.

Miami's population at the beginning of the year was 480.

Henry Flagler and Julia Tuttle were selling city lots for $300 to $900 apiece.

A lodge of Free and Accepted Masons was organized. It operated under dispensation until January 19, 1898, when it was chartered by the Florida Grand Lodge.

The First Presbyterian Church was established, and meetings were held in a tent-like structure which several denominations shared.

Miami's first theatrical experiment saw local talent producing minstral shows in an old shack.

1897   January 16. Henry Flagler opened his six-story Royal Palm Hotel, a yellow and white colonial structure complete with swimming pool. Guests would eventually include John D. Rockefeller, Vincent Astor, and Warren G. Harding.

Miami's first tourists arrived, including Mark Hanna and Philip Armour. Henry Flagler cut a channel across Biscayne Bay so guests could bring their yachts to the Royal Palm

Hotel docks.

A severe freeze threatened to destroy area farmers. Their survival was partially due to seed, fertilizer, and low-interest loans provided by Flagler.

The first County Fair in Florida was held in Miami under the direction of Rev. E. V. Blackman.

1898

February 3. Miami had its first civic organization, with the creation of the Board of Trade.

Spring. The first telephone company was established by J. R. Dewey with service being extended to a half-dozen customers.

April 5. The War Department announced placement of shore batteries in east coast cities including Miami, to ward off possible Spanish naval attacks.

May 19 & 25   Army officials visited Miami and rejected the small town as a camp site for Cuban War troops. Flagler, however, pursued efforts to secure such encampments.

June 20. Orders were issued for the transfer of some 7,500 troops to Miami. The town experienced difficulties accomodating so many troops, and the high incidence of diseases resulted in their removal within a month.

September 14. Julia Tuttle died in Miami at age 48.

Mid-September. A yellow fever epidemic struck Miami resulting in a three-month quarantine. Fourteen deaths occurred from a reported 263 cases.

Preparations for United States intervention in the Cuban War for Independence included formation of the Miami Minute Men.

1899

Spring. Miami suffered its second disastrous fire.

October 22. The State Health officer quarantined Miami because of a yellow fever epidemic. Flagler erected a hospital and paid for the services of nurses brought in to fight the disease.

The Miami Fire Department was organized.

The Dade County seat was moved permanently from Juno to Miami.

Congress appropriated funds for harbor improvements in Miami.

The town's first electric utility system appeared when Henry Flagler built a 45-kw gasoline-powered generator to supply electricity for street lights and private use. He added this facility to a small existing unit in his Royal Palm Hotel.

1900

January 15. The yellow fever quarantine was lifted after 220 cases and 14 deaths.

June 21. Miami became the chief terminal (until 1908) of Henry Flagler's newly organized Peninsular and Occidental Steamship Company.

November. J. E. Lummus was elected Miami's second mayor. He served three one-year terms.

Miami's population was 1,681, and Dade County's was 4,955.

The assessed valuation of Miami's personal and real property was $306,544.

The foundation of the city's public library was laid when the Married Ladies' Afternoon Club voted to contribute 10¢ a week to buy books for a reading room. This was the origin of Flagler Public Library.

The first wagon road was pushed through to Coconut Grove.

The building of the First Presbyterian Church was completed.

The Dade County Medical Association was organized with Dr. R. H. Huddleston as president.

1902

By an act of Congress, a plan was implemented through which the federal government and

Miami co-operated to begin work on Government Cut, a channel through Fisher's Island to the sea.

The First National Bank was opened.

1903   September 15. The Miami <u>Evening Record</u>, an evening daily, began publication.

November. John Sewell was elected mayor and served four one-year terms.

The Fort Dallas National Bank was opened.

The <u>Miami Metropolis</u> changed from a weekly to an eight-page daily newspaper.

1904   January 1. New Year's Day boat races were held on Biscayne Bay.

Dade County offices were opened in a new two-story stone building.

A new city power plant was constructed with two 100-KW generating units brought from a hotel in Nassau.

Henry Chase became Miami's first paid fireman, earning $45.00 a month.

Smith's Casino became the first bathing pavilion built on Miami Beach.

1905   Miami's population was 4,733.

The assessed valuation of Miami's personal and real property was $1,054,360.

Miami became a full-fledged port with completion of Government Cut, an 18-foot channel across Biscayne Bay.

S. Bobo Dean became editor of the <u>Miami Metropolis</u>, and what had been known as a "railroad organ" became a crusading anti-railroad paper.

The Miami Elks were organized as Miami Lodge, No. 948, B.P.O.E.

R. E. Hall succeeded Z. T. Merritt (1897-1905) as Superintendent of the Board of Public Education, a post he held for 16 years.

1906　　May 7. The Married Ladies' Afternoon Club became the Woman's Club of Miami.

July 4. The Tatum Brothers street car system inaugurated service, but it lasted only a year after which the tracks and cars were moved to another city.

A hurricane destroyed several sections of completed embankments constructed in order to extend Flagler's railroad to Key West. Perhaps as many as 200 workmen were killed.

The city's first movie theatre opened in the Hatchet Building on East Flagler Street.

1907　　July 5. Miami was shaken by the failure of the Fort Dallas National Bank. It resulted in part from the 1907 Panic, and in part from the failure of two large investments, the Halcyon Hotel, and the city's first street car system.

November. Frank H. Wharton was elected Miami's mayor and served two two-year terms.

Many in Miami avoided the worst effects of the national financial panic through the generosity of the Brickells, a family that did not believe in banks. Edith Brickell went about Miami loaning money from a large cache of bills in her bag. No notes were written.

The first fire station was built on land deeded to the city by Henry Flagler in 1903.

The "wets" defeated the "drys" in a local option election.

1908　　The Brickell family donated to the Board of Trade 200 building lots, and a block of land in the center of the city, with the understanding that proceeds from the lands' sale would be used to secure the establishment of cigar factories.

A group of aroused Dade County fruit growers led by the "Pineapple King", Miami's T. V. Moore, formed the East Coast Fruit and Vegetable Growers Association to fight discriminatory practices by the Florida East Coast Railroad. By 1910, the Association had won their fight.

Dan Hardie, the last of the frontier sheriffs, was chosen sheriff of Dade County. He wiped out the vice dens of North Miami.

1909

Temperance crusader Carrie Nation conducted a whirlwind campaign against alcoholic beverages.

The "wets" again defeated the "drys" in a local option election.

A new City Hall was constructed.

1910

December 10. The <u>Evening Record</u> became the <u>Miami Herald</u> under the direction of editor F. B. Stoneman.

Miami's population was now 5,471, with Dade County's at 11,933.

The assessed valuation of Miami's personal and real property was $1,508,097.

Over 400 citizens enjoyed telephone service.

Edward C. Romfh and his associates established the First Trust and Savings Bank (which became the Miami Savings Bank in 1918.)

Miami's electric facility was augmented with the addition of a 600-KW steam turbine.

Father A. B. Friend led a group which organized the Friendly Society. The Society then raised funds for a small hospital unit accommodating three beds.

1911

July 28. Miami, celebrating the 15th anniversary of its incorporation, paid Wright Brothers pilot Howard Gill $1,000 a day for an airplane demonstration.

November. Major Rodman B. Smith was elected mayor.

Central Grammar School was constructed. Miami's schools now served 282 Black, and 782 white children.

The first motor-driven fire-fighting equipment was purchased, and the department's personnel was increased to 12 men.

1912 January 22. A three-day celebration, complete with a circus imported from Cuba, marked the completion of Flagler's Florida East Coast Railroad to Key West.

Spring. Major Rodman Smith resigned as mayor due to ill health. John W. Watson was chosen to complete Smith's term.

June 3. The Miami Beach Improvement Co. was organized for the purpose of developing what would become Miami Beach. John S. Collins, the company's president, then began construction of a wooden causeway to the Beach and initiated land sales.

June 5. Another development company with interests in Miami Beach was chartered, the Ocean Beach Realty Company owned by the Lummus brothers.

Carl G. Fisher arrived in Miami and was impressed by the resort potential of what would be Miami Beach. He loaned John S. Collins sufficient money to complete Collins' planned bridge to the Beach. Fisher received 200 acres on the Beach in partial payment for his loan.

The Miami Municipal Airport was constructed by a company headed by Glenn Curtiss. It was the nation's third airport.

C. D. Brossier organized and became the first president of the Miami Realty Board.

The Friendly Society Hospital was incorporated as the Miami City Hospital.

1913 May. Henry M. Flagler died at age 82.

June 12. John S. Collins's two-mile wooden causeway to Miami Beach was formally opened.

November. John W. Watson was re-elected mayor.

Dade County voted to go "dry" by a count of 976 to 860.

The city began to burn coal instead of wood

to power its electric facility, and a 750-KW turbogenerator was added to the plant.

The "Vaudette" theatre was opened by a federation of laborers to supply "wholesome and low-cost entertainment."

The Woman's Club of Miami opened a public library on land donated by Henry Flagler.

1914   Building permits were issued amounting to $607,525.

The city began making annual appropriations to assist in the maintenance of the Woman's Club's public library.

The Miami Traction Company laid tracks for a new city transportation system.

1915   January 1. The Board of Trade and the Merchant's Association merged to form the Chamber of Commerce.

March 26. Miami Beach was incorporated as a town at a time when Carl Fisher was having trouble giving away land to anyone who would settle there.

May 13. The state legislature approved a new municipal charter for Miami.

November. Parker A. Henderson was elected to a two-year term as mayor.

Dade County's population was 15,592.

The assessed valuation of Miami's personal and real property was $13,251,400.

Building permits were issued in the sum of $769,040.

Captain J. F. Jaudon and Judge William F. Mill made the original proposal for the construction of the Tamiami Trail as a joint Lee-Dade County enterprise.

The city initiated work on a channel 105 feet wide and 18 feet deep from Government Cut to a turning basin that was 600 feet wide and 800 feet long. New port construction included a 1,000-foot concrete pier, a warehouse, and new rail facilities.

Miami spent $1,900 on its first municipal advertising campaign.

1916   July 16. Dade County floated the first of a series of bond issues to fund its share of the Tamiami Trail construction. This issue was for $275,000, and by 1924 subsequent issues would amount to another $325,000.

Building permits valued at $1,925,033 were issued.

The number of real estate transactions reached 9,956.

The assessed valuation of Miami Beach property was $224,000.

The city switched from dirty coal to Mexican oil to power its electric facility.

Glenn H. Curtiss established an aviation school.

The Southern Business College was founded by A. H. Perry.

The Business and Professional Women's Club was organized under President Marjory Stoneman Douglas.

Construction was completed on James Deering's muxurious $15 million, 300-acre estate, Viscaya.

1917   November. John W. Watson was again chosen to serve a two-year term as mayor.

A 1,500-KW turbine was added to Miami's electric utility plant.

Building permits were issued in the value of $1,250,925.

Real estate transactions numbered 11,288.

Telephones in service totaled 2,326.

The Miami City Hospital moved to a new 28-bed facility.

The Dinner Key United States Naval Aviation Base was established. It was moved shortly thereafter to Deering Island.

A YMCA Building was opened with $125,000 of primarily local contributions.

The Flagler Street bridge was opened, replacing a wooden structure.

1918 The number of real estate transactions was 8,114.

The federal government acquired the Curtiss Company's airfield, planes, and equipment as a center for training Marine Corps pilots. The facilities were returned to the Curtiss Company in 1919.

1919 March 5. Carl Fisher and other Miami Beach developers organized The Miami Beach Electric Company and the Miami Beach Railway Company.

September. W. J. Liddy took charge of the Southern Business College and changed its name to the Pan-American College of Commerce.

November. W. P. Smith was elected mayor.

Building permits valued at $3,155,165 were issued.

Real estate transactions totaled 14,258.

Coconut Grove was incorporated.

1920 January 1. The County Causeway was opened over Biscayne Bay to Miami Beach.

January 3. The Miami Realty Board was organized.

August 2. Bahama Blacks in Miami were aroused over the death of H. Brooks who had been charged with assaulting a white woman.

Miami's population was 29,571, which represented an increase of 440.5% over the 1910 figure. It was the largest percentage increase among American cities for that decade. Metropolitan Miami-Dade County's population (minus unincorporated areas) was 42,753.

The assessed valuation of personal and real property in Miami reached $58,963,450.

Building permits valued at $4,556,365 were issued.

The number of real estate transactions totaled 21,968.

Telephones in service numbered 3,653.

Threatened with the suspension of U.S. Mail Service, Miami changed its street names to provide an orderly system, and culled duplication of names and multiple names for the same street.

1921

January 21. A committee of 15 was selected to draft a new city charter based on the commission form of municipal government.

February. Fred W. Barton began operating Miami's first radio station, the 50-watt WFAW. The following year it became WQAM when the Miami Metropolis began aiding Barton.

June. Miamians approved a new city charter which provided for a commission-city manager form of government.

July 12. The "bankers' ticket," composed of five of the city's leading bankers, won election as the first five City Commissioners under the new charter. They chose Charles D. Loeffler as Commissioner-Mayor, and Colonel C. S. Coe as the first City Manager.

November 27. Promoter George E. Merrick sold the first lot in what would become Coral Gables, his "City Beautiful."

The assessed valuation of real and personal property in Miami stood at $63.820,000.

Building permits issued reached a record $5,415,800.

Real estate transactions numbered 24,242.

The first plan was prepared for the town of Hialeah.

Students in Miami's public schools totaled

9,153 and Charles M. Fisher succeeded R. E. Hall as Superintendent of the Board of Public Instruction. Fisher held the post until 1937.

Miami Studios, a motion picture company, was organized in Hialeah. It was the first step in a futile effort to make Miami the "Hollywood of the East".

1922

The assessed valuation of personal and real property reached $71,591,720.

Building permits were issued in the amount of $4,642,144.

Real estate transactions totaled 25,722.

The city purchased the remaining property of the Miami Traction Company whose car barns were destroyed in a 1921 fire.

Merrick's land sales in Coral Gables were about $1,400,000.

BOOM TIME IN MIAMI

1923

February 16. The Miami Chamber of Commerce prompted by the city's best tourist season, opened a bureau to help tourists locate accomodations.

March. The Miami Realty Board adopted the practice of multiple listing and organized a bureau that would handle the business.

The tourist season's high point was reached with the arrival of President and Mrs. Warren G. Harding. Other prominent visitors included Clarence Darrow, Harvey S. Firestone, J. C. Penny, and U. S. Senator T. Coleman Dupont.

The season's musical entertainment was provided by daily concerts from Arthur Pryor's band in Royal Palm Park, and by performances of such artists as Sergei Rachmaninoff, Madame Ernestine Schumann-Heink, Jascha Heifetz, and Geraldine Farrar.

March 20. City voters approved a $2,730,000 bond issue to finance park development along with railroad and hospital improvements.

May 8. The first city planning conference was held under the sponsorship of the Miami Woman's Club. It recommended amending the city charter to include a Planning Commission

May 20. The John B. Gordon Klan No. 24 (Ku Klux Klan) initiated 150 candidates on Palm Island. Thousands responded to a public invitation to view a Klan parade and ceremonies.

June 8. Work began on a new structure for the Bank of Bay Biscayne, Miami's largest and oldest bank.

June 9. The "bankers'" commission was re-elected to serve as City Commissioners. They chose Edward C. Romfh mayor and retained Frank H. Wharton as City Manager.

September 1. The Miami *Times*, a black weekly newspaper, was established.

November. In a typical publicity effort, the city extended itself to royally entertain the convention of the American Association of Traveling Passenger Agents.

December 1. With skyscrapers still a novelty, the 8-story Professional Building was opened with considerable public stir.

December 4. The "Floridian", the Illinois Central Railroad's luxury train, arrived in Miami, thereby successfully ending a seven-year fight for through train service between Miami and the mid-west.

Quickened activity in real estate circles marked the origins of the Miami land boom. Eighty-four subdivisions were recorded in Dade County with the majority being in the Miami area. Active subdivisions included Brickell Estates, Holleman Park, Shenandoah, Fulford, Hialeah and Coral Gables (where Merrick's sales amounted to about $4,000,000).

The assessed valuation of personal and real property stood at $77,461,835.

Building permits reached a record $7,201,266.

Real estate transactions numbered 34,549.

Steamship passenger service was inaugurated between New York and Miami.

Bayfront Park was developed from a mud-flat and Biscayne Bay.

Public school attendance was 11,733.

The U. S. Plant Introduction Bureau moved to Chapman Field from Brickell Hammock.

The tourist season featured William Jennings Bryan's first annual Tourist Bible Class, which met on Sunday mornings at Royal Palm Park.

1924

January. The Miami Clearing House was founded, and by mid-year had 7 member institutions with combined assets of $39,779,340.99.

February. At the Hialeah Jai Alai Fronton, forty Spanish athletes played the first Jai Alai seen in the United States.

March. The Florida East Coast Railroad announced plans to begin double-tracking its right-of-way from Jacksonville to Miami.

March 15. An announcement was made that the American Power and Light Company had purchased the Miami Beach Electric and Street Railway Companies, as well as other utilities in the Miami area. Miami city officials were delighted by the prospects of improved public services at reasonable rates.

April. The Miami Community Chest Association was organized and raised over $125,000 in a thirty-day campaign.

April 9. The Second Avenue Bridge across the Miami River was opened.

May 21. Miami voters approved a $950,000 capital improvements bond issue.

June. With real estate activity growing increasingly intense during the first half of the year, the *Miami Herald* became the world's leading newspaper in terms of advertising printed. The daily average was over 50 pages, and Sunday's edition commonly exceeded 100 pages.

Per capita wealth measured by bank deposits stood at $670, up from $170 in 1915.

June 30. Land sales in Coral Gables for the first half of the year were $7,326,920.52; for the year they totaled $13,705,879.59.

July. Dade County granted a franchise for a third causeway to Miami Beach. It was to be located at 79th Street. The following year voters decided to make it a public road.

August. Plans were announced for connecting Coral Gables and Miami by street-car.

September 8. The Miami Real Estate Board announced it would take steps to avoid illegitimate promotional campaigns for land sales in the Miami-South Florida area.

November 23. The arrival of the "Apache" in Miami Harbor marked the inauguration of Clyde Steamship Line passenger and freight service between Miami and New York.

December. The South Atlantic Telephone and Telegraph Company which had been serving Miami, sold out to Southern Bell Telephone and Telegraph, a division of the Bell system.

December 4. On this first day of land sales at Miami Shores, a corps of 75 salesmen sold lots worth $2,509,170.

Edward C. Romfh became Miami's Commissioner-Mayor.

Assessed property values reached $84,000,000. They had amounted to only $6,500,000 ten years before.

With the "Boom" gaining momentum, real estate transactions reached a total of 59,079.

Building permits valued at $17,038,164 were issued.

The number of persons filing income tax returns was up 33% over 1923.

Port activity included 58,229 cargo tons of imports and 4,972 cargo tons of exports.

The City engaged Warren H. Manning, a nationally known city planner, to prepare plans for park and waterfront improvements.

Forty acres of land, partially pumped from Biscayne Bay, were landscaped with tropical shrubbery and became Bayfront Park.

Miami's city hospital was renamed the James M. Jackson Memorial Hospital.

1925   January. William J. Bryan began his sales' lectures for George Merrick's Coral Gables.

Real estate along E. Flagler Street from Miami Avenue to Northeast Second Avenue commanded a minimum price of $10,000 per front foot. Seven years before, this land was available for $1,200 a front foot.

January 15. The first horse race was run at Hialeah.

March. The Federal Rivers and Harbors Act allocated $1,605,000 to improve Miami's shipping channel.

March 15. A local sensation was created by the murder of a popular police sergeant, Laurie L. Wever.

April 8. The state chartered the University of Miami. It began classes in October 1926 with 372 students and 15 faculty members under the direction of President Dr. Bowman F. Ashe. Its boom-time endowment of $8,500,000 was seriously depleted by the post-boom depression.

April 27. Coral Gables was incorporated.

May 20. New Silver Crest, a subdivision along Coral Way at 27th Avenue opened sales at 10:00 A.M. and sold out in 10 minutes. Over 200 lots were purchased at the rate of $750,000 a minute.

June. When no spring and summer lull occurred in Miami's population influx, a serious housing shortage developed. Particularly acute was the lack of low-cost housing for the laborers who were needed for the construction boom. Attempts to meet the demand ran afoul of the freight embargo imposed at a later date.

July 26. The Miami News published a 504-page, 7½ lb. edition, the world's largest single edition of a standard newspaper. It marked the opening of the News Tower and the city's 29th birthday. For the year, advertising lineage in the Miami Herald totaled 45½ million lines, almost 12 million lines ahead of its leading competitor in the U. S.

August 17. Because the Florida East Coast Railroad provided the only rail access to Miami, freight began to backup. Earlier embargos had not cleared the tracks. On this date the company embargoed all freight in carload lots except for fuel, oil, livestock, and perishable items. In one day there were 851 carloads of freight waiting on Miami sidetracks, with 150 cars outside the usual waiting areas. Over 700 cars were in transit, and traffic was backing up as far north as Jacksonville.

September. Miamians organized the Better Business Bureau to counteract the growing "anti-Florida" propaganda. Their efforts were directed at cleaning up unsavory business practices, especially among real estate men.

September 2. Miami expanded its borders as voters in surrounding communities approved annexation to the City of Miami. The communities included Coconut Grove, Silver Bluff, Lemon City, Buena Vista, Little River, and Allapattah.

September 3. The Shoreland real estate firm placed the Arch Creek tract of 400 acres on the market, and within 2½ hours received orders for $33,734,350 in property. That was an over-subscription of $11,319,650.

September 13. The last steamship line without restrictions on shipping placed all but the "necessities of life" under embargo. Now ships and trains were both shut off.

September 16. City employees and prisoners from the city jail assisted in the effort being made to clear freight congestion.

October. The "Boom" had peaked, though few had realized it.

A permit system was implemented to funnel "necessary" freight along the Florida East Coast Railroad.

December 2. By this date, land sales in Coral Gables reached $80,055,089.50, and construction begun during the year was valued at $207,800,000.

December 31. Figures from 8 large banks showed deposits of $173,375,856.05 which constituted an increase of 207.5% over 1924.

Miami's population was 84,258 which represented a 184.9% increase over 1920. Dade County's population was 111,332 up 161.1% over 1920 figures.

The assessed value of personal and real property was $188,829,024.

Building permits valued at $60,026,260 were issued, placing Miami 9th among U.S. cities of all sizes.

Telephones in service totaled 17,279.

Port activity included 193,127 cargo tons of incoming and 8,358 cargo tons of outgoing shipping.

Miami issued 7,500 licenses to real estate salesmen.

Frank H. Wharton became Miami's second City Manager.

The City of Hialeah was incorporated.

Members of the Miami Bus Association met and agreed to take on 20-passenger buses instead of jitneys. The Miami Transit Company placed motor buses in operation in January 1926.

The Seaborn Airline Railway was unable to buy a right-of-way into Miami until $1,500,000 in cash and land was given to the railroad. The contribution was the result of a mass rally called for that purpose by the Chamber of Commerce.

The School Board provided 150 one-room portable schools to serve the increased student population resulting from the "Boom."

The "Boom" and prohibition brought Miami more than its share of vice and crime, but city officials refused an offer from the Ku Klux Klan to police Miami.

With the "Boom" in full-swing, 971 subdivisions were plotted in the Miami area, and 176,530 real estate transactions were recorded. Land six and eight miles beyond the city limits was commanding $20-25,000 an acre. Building operations consumed 400 miles of awning material and 7,000 railroad carloads of lumber.

1926

January. With the real estate market declining and promoters seeking gimmicks to spur sales, the J. C. H. Corp. retained Pittsburgh Pirate baseball players such as Max Carey and "Pie" Traynor to sell land.

January 10. The "Prinz Valdemar", an old Danish naval training ship rigged as a floating hotel, went aground in the harbor, trapping 11 vessels in port and preventing others from entering. A channel was cut around it by early February.

January 15. The Miami-Biltmore Hotel was opened with great fanfare.

February 4. The cornerstone laying ceremony for the University of Miami was held.

February 22. With the freight lines unclogging, the Flordia East Coast Railroad partially lifted its embargo.

May 15. The last restrictions on freight shipments to Miami were removed.

June 30. The city's net bonded indebtedness was $21,348,000.

July. Another sign of the "Boom's" disappearance emerged when delinquent tax sales were held involving some 15,000 parcels of land.

CHRONOLOGY   25

July 1. Bank deposits were well of 1925 levels. For example deposits in the First National Bank amounted to $63,089,867.82 on September 28, 1925, and were only $31,917,487.38 on July 1, 1926.

September 2. Dredging began for harbor improvements based on the "Orr Plan."

September 17. At 11:00 A,M., storm warnings were posted because of an approaching hurricane.

September 18. Just after 12:00 A.M., the hurricane slammed into Miami with 130 m.p.h. winds that lashed the city for 8 hours. The storm abated as the "eye" passed over the city, and then it struck again, catching many people who had gone out to inspect the damage. Over 100 deaths occurred in Dade County, with hundreds more injured. Millions in property damage was also inflicted on Miami.

Recovery began rapidly with a nation-wide effort. In Miami, citizens' committees were given "dictatorial" powers within jurisdictions established in plans developed by Mayor Romfh and Florida's governor.

October 9. An announcement was made that 75% of the automobile tourists' camps would be closed as menaces to public health and morality.

Building permits reached a record high of $103,572,507.

The assessed valuation of property reached a "Boom" high of $389,648,391.

A paving company was busy laying $2,000,000 of streets for the expanding city.

Public school attendance totaled 31,770 students. Since 1923, 26 schools for whites and 6 for blacks had been constructed.

Several new communities were incorporated in the Miami area, including South Miami, Miami Springs, Miami Shores, and Opa-locka.

Radio station WMBF began broadcasting. It became WIOD and an NBC affiliate in 1929.

The Venetian Islands were constructed in Biscayne Bay.

DEPRESSION, WAR, AND PROGRESS

1927 January. The Seaboard Airline Railway reached Miami.

January 17. The Ministerial Association charged that civic bodies were influencing court decisions involving horse racing.

July 28. The Greater Miami Airport Association was formed.

August. The King of Miami's rum runners, Horace Alderman, killed two coast guardsmen and wounded another in a maritime battle off Miami. Two years later, he was hanged.

Work was complete which deepened Miami's shipping channel to 25 feet.

The "Prinz Valdemar", raised and beached after the hurricane, now became the Miami Aquarium.

1928 January 4. The first nonstop Miami-New York flight was made.

February 1. The City Commission organized an Aviation Department under the leadership of A. H. Hermance.

Spring. Federal agents arrested the notorious liquor runner, Spanish Marie, as she supervised unloading operations in Coconut Grove.

April 20. The Tamiami Trail was opened between Fort Meyers and Miami. It took 12 years to complete through the Everglades.

May 7. A Dade County Grand Jury denounced Miami Police Department policies as "tortuous."

September. Pan American Airways inaugurated service between Miami and Havana, after completing its airport in Miami.

CHRONOLOGY 27

September 6. A new 28-story Dade County Courthouse was opened.

Fall. Horse racing was stopped in Dade County.

November 6. For the first time since 1900, Dade County voters cast a majority of their ballots for a Republican presidential candidate.

E. G. Sewell became Miami's mayor.

The assessed property valuation was $317,675,298, down from the 1926 level of $389,648,391.

Pitcairn Aviation was founded. By 1934 it would be known as Eastern Air Lines.

The first All-American Air meet was held in Miami.

Miami hosted the National Shriner's Convention.

Al Capone purchased a private mansion on Palm Island between Miami and Miami Beach.

1929 June. The Miami Aero Club was formed.

September 19. A hurricane, whose fury centered on Key Largo, produced property damage in Miami but no deaths.

Redmond B. Gautier became Miami's mayor.

The assessed valuation of property continued to decline, standing now at $167,519,892.

1930 Spring. Miami adopted a new slogan: "Stay Through May," and began a concentrated effort to publicize the city and develop a summer tourist season.

May 23. A vagrancy ordinance aimed at Al Capone was passed. Under it, those without legal means of support could be arrested for vagrancy.

June. The Royal Palm Hotel, a symbol of luxury during Miami's early years, was condemned as unsound.

August 5. The city defaulted on interest and principal payments on its bonds. Banking houses advised creditors to accept new bonds in lieu of cash.

August 19. Controller E. Amod was cleared of charges of malfeasance in office.

Miami's population was 110,637, which represented a 31.3% increase over the 1925 level. Dade County's population had increased 28.4% in the same period and stood at 142,955.

Telephones in service numbered 29,000.

Building permits were issued in the amount of $2,159,496.

Miami's only bank was the First National Bank, all others having liquidated after the collapse of the "Boom" and/or with the onset of the depression.

Sewell Brothers, Miami's oldest existing business house, filed for bankruptcy.

The U.S. Navy established a Naval Reserve Base at Opa-locka.

Miami's economy continued to depend almost entirely on tourism. Manufacturing was practically nonexistent, and the leading industry outside tourism and construction was aviation.

1931

August. Alfred I. Dupont's Florida National Bank opened.

August 18. Chapman Field, a World War I air base, was reopened.

September 18. The Municipal Securities Association was appointed to design a refunding scheme to cure the city's financial woes.

November 11. A refunding bond issue was authorized by voters.

C. H. Reeder became Miami's mayor.

Building activity was up slightly over 1930, with building permits issued in the amount of $3,244,236.

Miami Shores and Biscayne Park were incorporated as municipalities on lands north of Miami. The city had annexed the area in 1925 but released it in 1930. The 1926 hurricane and later the depression, forced a reduction of city services and a contraction of boundaries.

Two horse racetracks were opened, the Hialeah Jocky Club and Tropical Park.

1932   June. Irate Miamians, upset by the refusal of city officials to adjust tax assessments after the post-1926 slump, formed the Citizens Taxation Committee to press for tax relief.

December 10. The University of Miami was placed in receivership.

E. G. Sewell again became Miami's mayor.

Building permits reached a depression low of $1,067,427.

Seeking new sources of funds, the city Commissioners aroused the ire of the citizenry with a proposal to license auto drivers for $1.00 on the basis of a written examination and no road test.

1933   February 15. In Bayfront Park, an attempt to assassinate President-elect Franklin D. Roosevelt resulted in the death of Chicago Mayor Anton J. Cermak.

July 19. The Bondholders Committee arrived at a tentative agreement with the city Commission on a plan to refinance the city's debt.

August 7. Bondholders dropped suits against the city after receiving payment in connection with the refinancing agreement.

A. D. H. Fossey was named Miami's mayor.

Building activity recovered somewhat; permits were issued worth $1,807,378.

The first extensive archeological project was launched in Dade County, and over 3,000 specimens taken from Indian mounds in Miami Beach and Opa-locka were sent to the Smithsonian Institution.

The first air-conditioned train reached Miami.

1934 The assessed valuation of Miami property stood at $97,871,000. It had been $389,648,391 in 1926.

The value of building permits was $2,810,092.

In an attempt to attract industry, the Chamber of Commerce created the Industrial Board. The Board cooperated closely with city officials who supplied $10,000 to publicize Miami and attract new industry to the area.

Miami became the nation's leading air gateway through the activities of Pan American and Eastern Air Lines.

A new Federal Building was dedicated.

The American Legion's National Convention was held in Miami.

The 1934-35 tourist season became the season "no wheels turned" when a series of violent incidents prevented politicians from giving the "go-ahead" to gamblers.

1935 January. Two men stole over $185,000 of jewelry from the hotel suite of Margaret Hawkesworth Bell. The resulting investigation disclosed corruption and bribery involving a number of policemen and officials.

February 19. Editor Paul G. Jeans and two others from the staff of the Miami Tribune were threatened with punishment for contempt of court in connection with their crusade against alleged corruption among public officials, vice protection, police misconduct, etc.

August 14. Mayor A. D. H. Fossey and two others were indicted on charges of obtaining property under false pretenses.

September 2. A Labor Day hurricane centering on the Keys killed over 300 men assembled by the federal government to construct a Miami-Key West highway.

December. A $2,000,000 harbor project was completed, enabling Miami to receive ocean liners drawing up to 30 feet.

Robert R. Williams became Miami's mayor.

Miami's population was 127,600, up 15.3% since 1930. Dade County's population was up 26.6% to 180,998.

Building permits valued at $5,515,940 were issued.

Telephones in service numbered 35,893.

An upswing occurred in real estate activity, and purchasers were covering city tax liens with city bonds that were selling at about 50% of face value.

During the 1935-36 tourist season, big time national gambling figures moved into the Miami-Miami Beach area, spreading a network of criminal-public official corruption.

The grandiose Royal Palm was opened as a front for gambling operations.

1936 Construction continued to improve with building permits valued at $12,614,824. Over $800,000 was spent on public works, an item on which nothing had been spent in 1935.

Port activity included 52,907 cargo tons of exports and 34,517 cargo tons of imports.

Dade County held its Centennial Celebration.

The Federal Housing Administration constructed a 20-acre low-cost housing project for Blacks at Liberty Square in Northwest Miami. It consisted of 34 apartment buildings.

1937 June 1. Amelia Earhart took off from Miami Municipal Airport on her ill-fated round-the-world flight.

October. During the 1937-38 (October-March) tourist season, Miami accomodated 796,000 visitors. Pari-mutual betting at Hialeah and Tropical Parks totaled over $44,000,000, while total visitor expenditures were about $60,000,000.

October 15. The Miami Herald Publishing Co. was purchased by J. S. Knight and associates.

Building permits were issued worth $14,003,604.

In Miami Harbor, 43,403 cargo tons were imported, and 61,140 cargo tons were exported.

There were 46,176 telephones in service, one for every 4.3 persons or 1.2 dwellings.

Of 55,721 homes, 94.3% were supplied with electricity.

Aviation continued to be an important industry. The industry's investment now exceeded $5.5 million.

James T. Wilse succeeded Charles M. Fisher as Superintendent of the Board of Public Instruction.

The city opened the Miami Public Library in the old post office building.

Roddy Burdine Stadium was opened and became the site of the annual Orange Bowl football game.

1938

January 17. A Special Grand Jury was impaneled to investigate the city administration.

January 24. Mayor Robert B. Williams, City Commissioners John DuBose and Ralph B. Ferguson, and two other city employees were indicted on bribery charges involving the Florida Power and Light Company and the Pitometer Company.

April 4. The Court ordered that Mayor Williams be tried on bribery charges.

October. Tourists between October 1938 and March 1939 spent about $67,000,000.

November 10. The Court ordered a recall election to be held for Mayor Williams and the City Commissioners on trial for bribery.

November 18. The city officials on trial were acquitted.

Bank deposits totaled $448,704,000 which was

almost double their 1934 level.

The value of building permits issued was $12,009,757.

Exports from Miami Harbor totaled 65,620 cargo tons, while imports totaled 39,658 cargo tons. United States Customs collections at the port reached $416,753.

Greater Miami boasted 190 churches and 11 hospitals with a capacity of 991 beds. There were also 28 municipal parks, 22 movie houses and one legitimate theatre.

The Police Department employed 255 men, and the Fire Department 177 men.

Four hundred and ninety-four manufacturing plants were located in the Miami area producing over 60 products. Aggregate employment in these plants was 6,882, and the annual payroll exceeded $8,000,000.

The 139-mile Overseas Highway was opened. Running from Miami across the Keys to Key West, it was built in part with a Reconstruction Finance Corporation loan of $3,000,000.

In the latter part of the year an exploratory oil well was sunk west of the city.

The Fleischer Movie Studios were opened.

The Ku Klux Klan held a public parade.

The first Seminole Pageant was held.

1939

March 1. In the city's first recall election, Mayor Williams and Commissioners Ferguson and DuBose were removed from office.

May 1. The Ku Klux Klan warned Blacks not to vote in the upcoming municipal election.

The Miami Daily News won a Pulitzer Prize for its fight against city corruption.

May 2. Blacks voted in the election to replace the recalled officials. Among the victors was the new mayor E. G. Sewell.

May 10. The state legislature passed a bill

barring Black voters from the primaries.

October. The 1939-1940 tourist season produced $82,385,000 in tourist expenditures.

New construction, as reflected in building permits, was valued at $16,825,532.

Harbor activity included 69,031 cargo tons of exports and 63,275 cargo tons of imports.

Miami contained 173 hotels and 9,678 rooms for rent.

A Grand Jury recommended transfer of Jackson Hospital from the City of Miami to Dade County, because of the hospital's financial inability to maintain either suitable facilities or the necessary equipment to discharge its functions.

Miami's Municipal Planning Board was created.

Miami public schools served about 46,000 students with 1,345 teachers. There were 89 schools in all, 68 for whites and 21 for blacks.

Diesel-powered electric train service was inaugurated between Miami and New York.

The first Tropical Festival was held.

1940

January. During "Palm Fete" week early in the month, an air meet was scheduled. The high point was a citywide blackout in preparation for a mock air raid.

January 11. Voters approved the city's purchase of the Miami Water Company.

April 2. Mayor E. G. Sewell died. He was replaced by Commissioner Alexander Orr Jr.

July 5. Miami contributed $5,000 to the American Red Cross war fund.

October. The 1940-1941 tourist season brought Miami $102,255,000 in tourist expenditures.

Miami's population was 172,172, up 34.9% since 1935, and Dade County's population was 267,739, up 47.9% over the 1935 level.

About 30,000 Blacks were now Miami residents, including some 5,000 Bahama natives who tended to be more sensitive to race prejudice than American Blacks. Job opportunities were usually limited to positions as servants and laborers.

Harbor activity included the exporting of 46,197 cargo tons, and the importing of 146,275 cargo tons.

Building permits valued at $15,214,518 were issued.

Tourist facilities including 186 hotels, 978 apartment buildings and 1,157 rooming houses.

Manufacturing still lagged, as employment statistics showed only 3.2% of the area's labor force involved in manufacturing, while 60.6% were employed in the wholesale and retail trades and the service industries.

Building remained the main non-tourist industry. The city boasted over 180 general and specialized contractors, and the industry employed 9.5% of the area's labor force.

Telephones in service numbered 76,550.

Busses replaced streetcars.

1941   October. The 1941-1942 tourist season produced over $111,000,000 in tourist expenditures.

Exports from Miami Harbor totaled 41,641 cargo tons, and imports totaled 101,764 cargo tons.

Royal Air Force cadets began studying navigation and meteorology in Miami. The University of Miami provided housing, food and classroom instruction, while Pan American Airways provided in-flight training.

1942   February 19. The tanker Pan Massachusetts loaded with 100,000 barrels of gasoline, oil and kerosene was blown up by a German submarine 20 miles south of Cape Canaveral.

May. German submarines sank a Mexican tanker

just off Miami

October. By now, one-fourth of the Army Air Force's officers and one-fifth of its enlisted men had been trained at Miami Beach.

Tourist expenditures for the 1942-1943 season reached $124,830,000.

Activity in Miami Harbor included the importation of 87,787 cargo tons of goods, and the exportation of 98,960 cargo tons.

Miami had 65,012 telephone units in service.

In 1942 and 1943, the Sub-Chaser Training School ("Donald Duck Navy") prepared about 10,000 officers and 37,000 enlisted men for U.S. service, along with 360 officers and 10,374 men for 14 other nations.

Pan American's Africa-Orient Division set up the "Cannon Ball Express" to fly cargo from Miami to Karachi, India for Burma and China. Over 14½ million miles were logged in less than a year.

The beginnings of the County Department of Public Health were established as Miami along with Miami Beach and Coral Gables turned over to the County funds appropriated for public health expenditures.

Miamians volunteered for civilian service in the Coast Guard auxillary for the Civil Air Patrol so they could aid in U-Boat spotting efforts.

1943   May 27. A County-wide public health system was created pursuant to an enabling act passed by the state legislature. It was the first in a series of pre-Metro steps, which involved increasing county-wide functional cooperation and consolidation.

June 14. The Greater Miami Port Authroity was created. It was actually a City of Miami agency and was given jurisdiction over harbors, ports and airports, along with the tunnels, causeways and bridges necessary to the operation of these facilities.

CHRONOLOGY 37

October. The 1943-1944 tourist season expenditures totaled $158,500,000.

Leonard K. Thomson became Mayor of Miami.

Dade County's population was 301,144, of which 63% lived in the City of Miami.

Exports from Miami Harbor totaled 116,841 cargo tons, while imports totaled 151,427 cargo tons.

There were 76,469 telephones in service.

With heavy industry still absent from the area, Miami ranked 103rd among U.S. manufacturing centers.

Barry College, an exclusive Catholic girls' school, was opened.

1944   August 22. The Dade County Coordinating Planning Council was organized to focus attention on area-wide, long-range problems. Though a failure, it was another of the pre-Metro advances made toward functional cooperation on a county-wide basis.

October. Tourist expenditures for the 1944-1945 tourist season totaled $175,935,000.

Exports from Miami Harbor totaled 66,028, and imports stood at 171,778 cargo tons.

There were 80,285 telephones in service in the city.

1945   April 3. A Dade County delegate to the state legislature refused to submit to that body Mayor Thomson's plan for consolidating all governmental units in Dade County into the "City and County of Miami."

June 11. The Greater Miami Port Authority was abolished in favor of the Dade County Port Authority. It was to be governed by the Board of County Commissioners and have jurisdiction within Dade County and beyond in the case of facilities which expanded beyond county boundaries.

September 15. At Richmond Base, 12 miles south of the city, 3 massive hangers burned after being struck by the eye of a hurricane. Stored inside the 16-story structures for protection against the storm were 14 inflated and 11 deflated blimps, 366 airplanes, and 150 cars.

October. Tourist expenditures for the 1945-1946 tourist season totaled $193,528,500.

October 2. Dade County voters approved consolidation of the area's 10 school district into a single school system controlled by the County Board of Public Instruction. The vote was 13,800 to 821.

October 25. The Orange Bowl Stadium was ordered sold, and plans for a new 100,000-seat facility were revealed.

Perrine Palmer, Jr. became Miami's mayor.

Miami's population stood at 197,326, up 14.6% since 1940. During the same period, Dade County's population was up 17.7% to 315,060.

Exports from Miami Harbor totaled 66,811 cargo tons, while imports totaled 225,278 cargo tons.

Telephones in service numbered 94,694.

1946

January 1. The Dade County Port Authority purchased Pan American Airway's 36th Street airport for $2,464,598.

February 26. Winston S. Churchill received an honorary degree from the University of Miami.

May 7. The freeholders of Dade County approved the transfer of Jackson Memorial Hospital from the City of Miami to Dade County by a vote of 28,205 to 3,843.

June 30. Miami's International Airport led the nation in foreign air commerce for the fiscal year ending June 30, 1946, handling 42% of all air imports and exports going through U.S. air terminals.

October. Tourist expenditures during the 1946-1947 season totaled $220,622,500 at a time when the city's accommodations included

512 hotels, 2,953 apartments, 2,378 rooming houses, 142 motor courts, and 27 auto trailer camps. Their total capacity was 150,000 visitors.

The assessed valuation of the City of Miami was $240,921,220, up almost $100,000,000 from 1937. Dade County's assessed valuation stood at $795,200,000, which was over $400,000,000 above the 1937 figure.

Building permits issued in Metropolital Miami were valued at $71,788,946, a 20-year high.

Commercial construction began to pick up after a World War II standstill. Over $15,000,000 worth of work was initiated on 218 stores, 51 office buildings, 2 large warehouses, and other projects.

Bank deposits in Dade County totaled $438,000,000; they had been $75,000,000 in 1939.

Harbor activity included 303,317 cargo tons of imports and 45,572 cargo tons of exports.

Miami's public school system consisted of 68 schools for white and 13 schools for Black children. There were also 5 parochial institutions.

There were 115,274 telephones in service.

The aviation industry in Miami employed 14,530 people with a payroll of $50,288,656. Non-payroll expenditures by the industry totalled $20,124,140.

Control of the Miami Yacht Basin was separated from the Port of Miami, and placed under the Department of Yacht Docks and Small Craft.

Bayfront Auditorium hosted 102 conventions and trade shows, attracting 469,853 visitors who spent over $10,000,000 in the city.

Construction was begun on the new Main Campus of the University of Miami.

1947   January. Businessmen created and financed a "good government" group known as the Dade

County Research Foundation to act as a "watchdog" over governmental activities.

July 21. A 5% tax on hotel and apartment bills for transient guests was adopted despite considerable protest.

November 27. Robert C. Floyd was elected Miami's mayor. At 29, he was the city's youngest mayor ever.

Post-war construction continued to boom as the number of new dwelling units constructed increased by 123% over the 1946 level.

Miami's airports handled 1,034,174 passengers and 33,362,006 pounds of air freight.

West Miami incorporated as a municipality to prevent annexation by Miami.

A grand jury report estimated that Jackson Memorial Hospital was costing the city $600,000 annually. Despite this information, and the May 1946 Dade County vote, the city still refused to turn the hospital over to the county.

A survey revealed the need for $2,000,000 worth of repairs for the Port of Miami, but over the next 7 years only $633,000 was spent.

Construction was completed on the $6,000,000 Rickenbacker Causeway connecting Miami, Virginia and Biscayne Keys.

A second deck was added to the Orange Bowl Stadium at a cost of $1,250,000. Seating capacity was increased from 23,000 to 60,000.

1948

January 24. The *Miami Herald* became sole owner of radio station WQAM by purchasing Fred Barton's interest.

March 31. The Greater Miami Crime Commission, a citizen's group, was founded. It was formed by 250 delegates representing Dade County civic, patriotic, and business organizations at a 3-day law enforcement conference at the Mayfair Theatre.

April. A diarrhea epidemic swept Jackson Memorial Hospital leading to a number of infant deaths. A subsequent investigation again revealed the hospital's need for funds and facilities.

May 25. Dade County voters rejected an amendment to the state constitution, which would have created "Miami County" out of Miami, 3 small towns, and unincorporated areas of Dade County. The vote was 27,821 to 23,513.

June. Petititons were circulated requesting a recall election for Mayor Floyd and the City Commissioners, after they had voted to dismiss City Manager Richard G. Danner.

June 2. The City Commission voted 3-2 to transfer Jackson Memorial Hospital to Dade County.

August. Elizabeth Virrick led a crusade to clean up Black slums in Coconut Grove.

August 5. The City Commissioners approved a 1% gross receipts levy on newspapers and periodicals which most people saw as retaliation for the part the press had played in the recall movement against the Mayor and Commissioners.

August 18. The tax on newspapers and periodicals was nullified.

November. Freeholders in Dade County approved a bond issue of $2,250,000 to expand Jackson Memorial Hospital.

Miami building permits were valued at over $30,000,000, while Dade County's totaled $65,903,000.

Walter Headley, an ex-cavalryman, became the city's Police Chief.

1949   September. The City Commission chose a portion of Bayfront Park as the location for the new Public Library structure.

William M. Wolforth became Miami's mayor.

Dade County boasted over 400 manufacturing establishments, which employed over 10,000 workers. The payroll exceeded $10,000,000 and gross business receipts were about

$25,000,000.

Wearing apparel was one of Miami's leading industries. There were over 50 firms in the area employing about 2,000 workers with a payroll of $2,800,000.

The approximate assessed valuation of Miami was $462,000,000, and that of Dade County was $892,700,000.

There were over 60,000 students in Miami public schools, and the school budget exceeded $18,000,000.

The Dade County legislative delegation in Tallahassee secured enactment of a measure that prohibited further incorporations in Dade County under the state's general municipal incorporation law. Incorporation was now possible only through an act of the legislature.

1950   October. Dade County Sheriff "Jimmy" Sullivan was indicted by the Dade County grand jury in connection with local gambling activity. The indictment was later dismissed by the State Supreme Court.

Miami's population was 249,276, up 26.3% since 1945. Metropolitan Miami's population was 495,084, up 57.1% over 1945.

Miami's airports serviced 1,387,142 passengers and handled 71,871,367 pounds of air freight.

Miami's labor force totaled 199,838, an increase of 91.4% over the 1940 level. The city's economic base is apparent from the fact that 62% of the labor force was employed in the retail and wholesale trades and service industries.

An ordinance was passed permitting the creation of the Slum Rehabilitation and Prevention Bureau.

The Kefauver Crime Investigating Committee of the U.S. Senate held hearings in Miami with a special eye toward organized gambling in Miami and Florida.

1951   May 7. The *Miami Herald* won a Pulitzer Prize for its 1950 investigative reporting on syndicate crime control over Miami gambling.

September 22. A dynamite blast shook Carver Village in what was viewed as a protest against the opening of its apartments to black residents.

November 28. Chelsie J. Senerchia was elected Mayor of Miami.

December 2. Three dynamite blasts, the latest in a series, rocked the city and aroused demands for police action. One of the blasts hit the Carver Village housing project, another the Hebrew School and Congregation, and a third went off in a residential area.

December 3. Mayor Senerchia conferred with Police Chief Headley on the bombings. A $5,000 reward was offered for information leading to an arrest, and $10,000 was appropriated for an investigation.

December 7. The FBI began investigating the Miami bombings for possible violations of federal laws.

December 9. A stick of dynamite tossed at the Coral Gables Jewish Center failed to explode.

December 25. Harry T. Moore, state coordinator of the NAACP, was murdered in an explosion which ripped through his residence in Mims, Florida. Miami officials speculated on a possible connection with the recent city bombings.

The Inter-American Cultural and Trade Center Authority (Interama) was appointed to build and operate a trade and cultural center.

1952   November 4. Dade County voted for the Republican presidential candidate, Dwight D. Eisenhower.

Dade County voters approved by 53,830 to 44,596 a permissive home-rule amendment to the state constitution, but the state-wide vote went against the amendment by 232,741 to 175,117.

Aroused by the recent bombings, concerned citizens formed the Dade County Council of Community Relations to deal with race problems. It would be given much of the credit for desegregating the public schools without major trauma.

Aggressive municipal planning was undertaken with the hiring of a technical consultant and staff to aid the Planning Board in developing a master plan.

1953　June 9. In a city-wide referendum, voters narrowly rejected a proposal to abolish the city government and transfer its functions to Dade County. The vote was 26,692 to 27,600. Their slim margin of victory made opponents of consolidation aware of the need for concessions.

July 1. The City Commission voted 3-2 to create the Metropolitan Miami Municipal (3M) Board and allocated $50,000 for the study of municipal and county governments in Dade County, and the drafting of a plan for their consolidation or federation.

December 7. The collapse of a municipal pier emphasized once again the degenerated condition of the waterfront.

Abraham Aronovitz became mayor of Miami.

Municipal piers handled 264,997 tons of cargo and 84,000 passengers.

The city hosted 3,500,000 tourists and temporary visitors.

The state legislative delegates from Dade County arrived at an informal agreement to block special legislative acts creating new cities in the county.

1954　March 9. The University of Miami's Committee on Municipal Research accepted a contract from the 3M Board to supervise a fact-finding survey of metropolitan area governments.

May. Area-wide newspapers intensified criticism of the Dade County Commissioners for alleged abuses in connection with the Port Authority and county business transactions.

December 31. Working on a contract from the University of Miami's Committee on Municipal Research, the Public Administration Service (Chicago) issued a report which recommended a federal form of government for the metropolitan area.

1955 January 14. The 3M Board approved the Public Administration Service's report and proceeded in cooperation with the Dade delegation to the state legislature to draft a home rule amendment to the state constitution.

June. The state legislature approved the home rule amendment to the state constitution and directed that it be submitted to a statewide vote in the November 1956 general elections.

June 23. The first Charter Board was created by the state legislature. Consisting of nineteen members, including seven from the 3M Board, it was to present a home rule charter to the Dade County Commissioners by October 1, 1956. They, in turn, would present the charter to the county's voters in the November 1956 general elections.

August 26. The first Charter Board decided that the home rule charter would guarantee the autonomy of all municipalities in Dade County.

November. Mayor Abe Aronovitz resigned and was replaced by Randall N. Christmas.

Miami's population was 259,035, while that of Metropolitan Dade County was 703,777.

The Miami Chamber of Commerce became the Miami-Dade Chamber of Commerce.

1956 May 28. A Florida Circuit Court declared the proposed home rule amendment unconstitutional on the grounds that it revised more than one article of the state constitution and was so confusing as to be unintelligible to voters.

June 26-28. The first Charter Board conducted public hearings on a proposed home rule charter.

August 9. The state legislature created a

second Charter Board which superseded the first. New legislation also dictated that Dade County voters would not vote on the home rule amendment and a proposed home rule charter at the same time in November 1956. If the amendment passed, voting on the charter would come later.

September 7. The Florida Supreme Court upheld the constitutionality of the proposed home rule amendment.

November 6. The home rule amendment was approved in a state-wide election, 322,839 to 138,430. In Dade County, the count was 86,612 for and 34,437 against. Thus, the constitutional basis was provided for Miami-Dade County metropolitan government.

Dade County voters again chose the Republican candidate Dwight D. Eisenhower in the presidential election.

MIAMI UNDER METRO

1957

January 1. A new 5-man Dade County Commission took office. Later in the year, it would become the first Metro Commission.

January 10. The second Charter Board reaffirmed the principle of autonomy for purely local matters.

April 2-4. The second Charter Board conducted public hearings on a proposed home rule charter.

April 15. The final draft of the home rule charter was signed by the members of the second Charter Board.

April 29. A Special Committee of the Dade League of Municipalities recommended to their membership that the League oppose the home rule charter.

May. The County Commissioners authorized county lawyer Marion E. Sibley to draft ordinances which would spell out the basic relationship between the proposed metropolitan government and the municipalities.

CHRONOLOGY

May 9. The 3M Board voted 14-1 to endorse the proposed home rule charter.

May 21. Dade County voters approved the home rule charter by a vote of 44,404 to 42,620 when only 26% of the registered voters went to the polls. "Metro" was a reality.

July 9. County attorney Marion E. Sibley released a list of proposed changes in county government to be implemented with the home rule charter. Officials of several cities, including Miami, charged that the changes were aimed at destroying municipal autonomy, and a struggle was begun which, over the years, would define the relationship between Metro and local governments.

July 21. Metro government was officially launched.

July 22. O. W. Campbell accepted the position of Dade County Manager.

August 12. The Dade League of Municipalities began circulating a petition calling for a home rule charter amendment which would ensure local autonomy.

August 16. The County Commission enacted a public works ordinance that established minimum standards that all cities had to meet for public works projects. Several cities protested vehemently.

September 16. The County Commission enacted a metropolitan traffic code which produced severe criticism and even non-compliance by several municipalities.

O. W. Campbell arrived to assume his duties as Dade County Manager and Metro's chief administrator.

October 3. A Mutual Aid Agreement was adopted by the County and most cities in the Greater Miami area, providing better emergency fire protection.

October 11. The Dade County Research Foundation warned that the proposed autonomy amendment to the home rule charter would jeopardize Metro's future.

MIAMI

October 16. The Dade League of Municipalities filed petitions with the County Commission which contained 38,002 signatures in support of a referendum on the autonomy amendment.

October 24. A group of 20 Miami businessmen and professionals calling themselves the Committee to Stop Double Taxation proposed to the County Commission the abolition of the City of Miami. The Commission called for a referendum on the question.

October 29. By ordinance, the County Commission adopted the South Florida Building Code.

November 12. Circuit Judge William A. Herin refused to enjoin a referendum on the question of abolishing the government of the City of Miami.

November 13. Acting at the behest of the group which had made the initial proposal, the County Commission withdrew the resolution calling for a referendum on the abolition of Miami's government.

December 2. County attorney Darrey A. Davis announced he was working with the Dade League of Municipalities on a compromise autonomy amendment to the home rule charter.

December 12. The Miami-Dade Chamber of Commerce met with all parties involved in the autonomy amendment controversy, and together they drafted a compromise version.

December 13. The County Commission rejected the compromise version of the autonomy amendment.

December 15. The 14-story Dupont Plaza Center was opened downtown. It included a 301-room hotel and an office building. It was part of an attempt to rejuvenate downtown.

December 19. The League of Women Voters came out against the autonomy amendment.

Robert King High became mayor of Miami.

1958   January 1. The Dade County Research Foundation went on record against the autonomy amendment.

February 5. A Circuit Court decision postponed the referendum election on the autonomy amendment until the Florida Supreme Court could rule on the constitutionality of the proposed amendment.

February 27. City of Miami attorney William L. Pallot organized a committee of civic and government leaders to make another attempt at working out a compromise autonomy amendment.

March 8. Plans were announced for a $20,000,000 port to be located on islands in Biscayne Bay.

March 16. At 2:30 A.M. a bomb blast rocked Miami's Temple Beth El school annex.

June 27. Circuit Court Judge Pat Cannon ruled that the municipalities had to enforce the Metro traffic code. In essence, the decision confirmed the pro-Metro interpretation of the wide powers conferred on Metro by the home rule charter.

July 23. The Florida Supreme Court ordered the autonomy amendment referendum to be held.

July 31. The County Commission set September 30 for the autonomy amendment referendum.

August 9. Forty-six candidates qualified for the six County Commission seats.

September 9. None of the 46 candidates received a majority vote in the election for County Commission seats, necessitating a runoff on September 30.

September 19. Miami Mayor Robert High protested to City Manager E. E. Evans about the printing of pro-autonomy amendment posters by the city. All the City Commissioners, except the mayor, supported the autonomy amendment, as did the city employees who were led to believe that failure of the amendment would mean the end of their jobs.

September 30. The autonomy amendment was defeated by a count of 48,893 for, and 74,420 against.

Six new City Commissioners were chosen.

October 7. The County Commission voted 4-0 to kill an ordinance which would have legalized gambling casinos and slot machines in Dade County.

December 17. The Florida Supreme Court upheld the legality of the Metro traffic code and traffic court system.

Manufacturing was still not an economic strength of Greater Miami. Only 13 percent of the area's non-agricultural labor force was employed in manufacturing, while about 30 percent of the national labor force was so employed.

1959

January 15. Paul C. Watt became the Metro Planning Director.

January 21. The County Commission named eleven civic leaders to Metro's first Planning Advisory Board.

February 9. The County Commission passed a Metropolitan Dade County Urban Renewal Ordinance which provided for rehabilitation, clearance and redevelopment of slums and decayed areas in Dade County.

February 23. A decision by Circuit Court Judge Ray H. Pearson upheld Metro's authority to regulate liquor sale hours, motor vehicle inspection, tradesmen licensing, traffic control devices, building codes, sewage collection and disposal, and water supply. This decision was upheld by the State Supreme Court on November 13, 1959.

March. Efforts by the County Commission to purchase three bus lines were stalled over the question of price. The three lines carried almost 85 per cent of Dade County's transit passengers.

March 2. Miami City Manager Evans was fired by a 3-2 vote of the City Commission, and Commissioner James W. High resigned in protest. Ira F. Willard replaced Evans.

March 4. The City of Miami Commission approved the use of Metro car inspection stickers.

March 20. After charging that some County Commissioners were trying to undermine metropolitan government, Harry T. Toulmin resigned as Metro's Budget Director.

April 20. County Manager Campbell fired the new Budget Director, James Picola, after the latter suggested Campbell's office was top-heavy with overpaid administrators.

May 11. In a decision handed down by Circuit Court Judge Robert H. Anderson, the City of Miami was ordered to refund more than $1,000,000 collected from traffic violators after the Metro traffic code went into effect on March 1, 1958. On November 4, the State Supreme Court upheld Anderson's decision that the Miami traffic court was without jurisdiction, but reversed the order to refund fines collected.

May 29. Miami's City Commission informally approved a referendum on a proposal to transfer to the County Commission the governmental functions carried out under the city's charter.

July. Metro's Planning Department recommended that a new seaport be built on Dodge Island. It was unclear whether the city or county government would finance it.

August 15. The Dade County Board of Public Instruction accepted 4 black applicants to Miami's Orchard Villa school, making that school the first integrated public school in Florida. Most white residents moved out of the district.

September 2. The City Commission tabled the proposal to merge Miami with the Metro government.

September 3. Twenty-three blacks enrolled at Orchard Villa school.

October. Miami announced it would sell the 1,700-acre plot called the Graves Tract and use the money to build the Dodge Island seaport.

December 22. *Miami Herald* reporter J. C. Buchanan escaped a sentence of 14 years hard labor in Castro's Cuba by agreeing to leave the island in 24 hours.

1960

January 15. Racial integration was ordered at the city's police training school.

February 1. Ira Willard resigned as Miami's City Manager.

February 12. Mayor High charged that numbers racketeers were paying policemen $10,000 a week for protection. He urged the suspension of Police Chief Headley and the institution of a grand jury probe.

March 21. Melvin L. Reese was appointed Miami's new City Manager.

The Civil Service Board repealed bars against the promotion of blacks in the police force.

April 1. An agreement was reached between Metro and the City of Miami whereby Metro would construct and operate the new Dodge Island seaport.

May 3. Dade County freeholders approved a $46,000,000 expressway bond issue to complete the area's projected road system by 1966.

July 1. Metro absorbed all Dade County's municipal traffic engineering departments.

July 5. A 5-man Metropolitan Dade County Water and Sewer Board was created with a view toward centralizing the water and sewage systems in Metro's jurisdiction. At the time, there were some fifty-seven water and sewage companies in Dade County, and most Dade residents had septic tanks.

August 2. A Metro ordinance created the Metropolitan Dade County Transit Authority and provided for the purchase, development and operation of adequate mass transit by the county.

October 14. The *Miami Herald* ran a feature story saying County Manager Campbell would resign in January 1961, when he apparently had never indicated that he intended to do so.

November 14. Mayor High presented the Key to the City to President-elect John F. Kennedy.

November 20. Metro's Planning Department presented a preliminary land-use program for Dade County.

Miami's population was 291,688, up 17% since 1950, while Metropolitan Dade County's figures were up 88.9% in the same period to 953,047.

Miami's port handled 2,250,000 tons of general cargo and 155,000 passengers.

1961   January 17. The Metro Commissioners directed the Transit Authority to purchase Mr. Pawley's three bus lines for $7,705,274. The companies involved were the Miami Transit Company, the Miami Beach Railway Company, and the South Miami Coach Lines.

February 3. Four blacks sought admission to the University of Miami.

February 14. O. W. Campbell was fired as Dade County Manager.

March 7. An arrangement for the purchase of four water companies was rejected by the Metro Commissioners.

April 6. Irving C. McNayr was named Dade County's new County Manager.

May 9. The Metro Commission approved the contract for the purchase of Pawley's bus lines.

May 22. John McLeod, a former Commissioner, submitted to the Metro Commission an initiative petition (64,000 signatures) that requested a referendum on what would be known as the McLeod Amendment. It was a series of thirty-nine proposed changes in the home rule charter that would have seriously altered the nature of metropolitan government. The vote was scheduled for October 17, 1961.

June 10. The University of Miami accepted black students at its Coral Gables campus.

Summer. The summary dismissal of Melvin Reese as City Manager aroused a great public stir in Miami. An intense mass media campaign was followed by Reese's reinstatement during a dramatic televised ceremony.

August 15. Dade County voters approved by 10 to 1 the repeal of the home rule charter provisions which called for reassessment of all real and tangible property in the county. When the new tax roles were prepared, with about 80% assessments, residents were outraged.

October 17. A survey conducted by the University of Miami Government Department revealed that very few people knew anything about the McLeod Amendment.

October 17. Dade County voters rejected the McLeod amendment by 97,170 votes for and 105,097 votes against.

November 21. Mayor High was re-elected.

1962

January 29. A strike was initiated against the Pawley bus lines.

February 6. The Metro Commissioners decided to finance the construction of recreational facilities in the county's unincorporated areas.

February 9. Metro formally took possession of the Pawley bus lines at 12:01 A.M. Metro and the drivers' union were unable to reach an agreement on whether the union had the right to bargain with or strike against the government. The strike, therefore, continued, and the Transit Authority began hiring new drivers as civil servants. By March, normal service was returning, but embittered relations remained between Metro and organized labor.

February 20. This day was officially chosen as the day when Greater Miami achieved a population of 1,000,000. "Mr. Million" moved to Phoenix, Arizona three months later.

February 28. Metro and the City of Miami agreed to hold monthly joint meetings to decide which functions might best be handled on a county-wide basis, and which should be jointly handled by both governments.

May 8. A referendum on a proposition to repeal the Metro ordinance authorizing a bond issue to buy the bus lines was defeated by 82,394 to 47,268. The initiative petition had been inspired by the bus drivers' union.

June 11. President Roberto Francisco Chiari of Panama was presented a gold Key to the City.

August 21. A referendum election was held on the five so-called Crandon amendments to the home rule charter. The product of a committee headed by Charles H. Crandon, the amendments represented a challenge to Metro's wide powers. Only 16.6% of the electorate voted, and the only two amendments approved did not dent Metro's powers or alter its relationship to the municipalities.

August 24. County Manager McNayr was given a vote of confidence by the County Commission, something he requested after the two successful Crandon amendments reduced the County Manager's powers.

Later the same day, McNayr spectacularly resigned over another dispute with the County Commission.

August 31. McNayr withdrew his resignation at a special televised County Commission meeting.

Fall. Several members of a far-right organization, the Florida States Rights Party, were arrested, tried, convicted and jailed in connection with a series of bombings and bomb threats against supporters of integration and the Community Relations Board.

Members of the Dade County Teachers Association (Black) and the Dade County Classroom Teachers Association (white) voted to merge.

In a city notorious for the lack of individual and group civic leadership, the Government Research Council of the Miami-Dade Chamber of

Commerce was the sole continuously functioning organization among businessmen which was concerned exclusively with broad governmental problems.

1963   June. The first joint professional association meeting of white and **Black** teachers was held at Convention Hall in Miami Beach.

October 4. By now, Cuban registrants at the Cuban Refugee Center numbered 168,897.

November 5. Voters approved amendments to the Metro charter that called for eight Commissioners and a weak mayor to be elected on an at-large basis, though the Commissioners had to reside in different districts. In another contest, voters approved making the sheriff's post elective.

The County Commission passed an enabling ordinance for the creation of an 18-member Community Relations Board to encourage bi-racial communication in Dade County.

Work was begun on an urban renewal project in downtown Miami, the first such undertaking in Dade County. The project was aimed at the central black area in downtown Miami.

1964   January 28. Dade County voters rejected 59,950 to 48,490 a proposed charter amendment sponsored by opponents of urban renewal. It would have required all programs to be approved by the voters of the municipality or unincorporated area effected, and all funds to be raised within the jurisdiction effected.

About 350 new industrial plants and major expansions occurred in Greater Miami, bringing the number of area manufacturing concerns to 3,200. The expansion meant 4,500 new jobs for the 420,000-man labor force and allowed Dade County to lead the nation in the rate of increase in manufacturing plants, employment, payrolls, and value added by manufacturers.

There were over 300 active and militant anti-Castro groups in Miami.

1965   November 16. Mayor Robert King High was re-elected.

CHRONOLOGY   57

December 1. The twice daily freedom flights from Havana were initiated.

Over fifty of Dade County's 206 public schools were integrated, with 5,000 of the area's 38,000 black students enrolled in formerly all-white schools.

1966   February. A Metro progress report submitted to the state legislature by the Dade County delegation, a generally pro-Metro group, concluded that Metro had not lived up to expectations.

February 25. The University of Miami expelled two students and disciplined fifty-one others in a cheating scandal.

April 11. Dr. Martin Luther King arrived in Miami and noted that his Southern Christian Leadership Conference researchers had found "hostility and alienation: in the city.

April 20. Communist scholar-writer Herbert Aptheker was hanged in effigy as he gave a lecture to a University of Miami student group.

Dade County Sheriff Buchanan was suspended and charged with perjury and failure to report $25,000 in campaign contributions allegedly received from policy operators. Buchanan blamed the charges on a <u>Miami Herald</u> series concerning connections between gamblers and the police.

October 22. Three white youths were attacked and stabbed while "looking around" in a black district. One died.

1967   August 30. Mayor Robert King High died.

September 2. The City Commission named Vice Mayor William Clark to fill the mayor's office until the November election.

October 2. An 18-month University of Miami study, funded by the U. S. Department of Health, Education and Welfare and the Ford Foundation, found that the Cuban refugees were an economic and cultural asset to Miami far outweighing the initial problems created by their arrival.

November. William Clark was elected Mayor of Miami.

December 26. Angered by an outburst of crime and violence during the Christmas weekend, Police Chief Headley declared "war" on lawbreakers in the city's Black districts. Stepped up patrol activity was coupled with the use of shot guns and dogs to check crime.

December 27. NAACP leaders demanded the resignation of Chief Headley.

December 29. Headley defended his "get tough" policy to the City Commission and received its general support, although Commissioner Maurice Ferre scored Headley for the "inflammatory" way he announced his policy. The ACLU announced it would seek a Federal Court injunction against Headley.

1968

January 5. The Community Relations Board asked Chief Headley to elaborate on his "get tough" policy and restate his March 1967 pledge to enforce the law impartially.

January 14. Police figures indicated Headley's "get tough" policy had produced a 60-65% drop in crimes of violence.

February 3. One white Miami policeman resigned, and another was suspended after the two allegedly stripped a Black youth and dangled him from a highway overpass.

April 17. Chief Headley stated that arsonists and looters should be shot on sight during a riot.

May 14. Fourteen black University of Miami students were arrested when they refused to vacate the President's office after presenting demands for increased "blackness" on campus.

July 6. The Miami-Dade Chamber of Commerce invited a number of civil rights, labor, and ethnic groups to become members.

July 19. The Federal Aviation Administration noted that Miami-Dade Junior College had the first college training program for traffic control specialists.

August 7. With the Republican National Convention meeting across the Bay in Miami Beach, racial violence flared in the Liberty City district. Several people were injured as fires and looting spread through the area.

August 8. The violence continued as three blacks were slain in gunfire exchanges between rioters and police. Scattered incidents also occurred in the center city and Coconut Grove black areas. Governor Kirk sent 950 National Guardsmen to the city, and a 6:00 P.M. to 6:00 A.M. curfew was imposed on a 500 block area.

August 9. Relative calm was restored to the riot areas.

August 10. Miami and Dade County officials agreed to release without bond 250 Blacks arrested during the disorders and to send medical teams into Liberty City to treat tear gas victims, and in return, Black leaders pledged to try to ease tensions.

August 13. The curfew was lifted, and National Guardsmen and the Dade County Sheriff's forces were withdrawn from Liberty City. City Manager Melvin Reese appointed two Black aides to establish closer liason between City Hall and the "troubled areas."

September 4. The coroner ruled that the police were justified in shooting two Blacks during the August riot. The death of a third Black man was still under investigation.

September 10. Two former policemen pleaded no contest in federal court to a charge of violating the civil rights of a Black youth by dangling him naked from a highway overpass, and threatening to drop him.

November 16. Police Chief Walter Headley died and was replaced by Bernard L. Garmire.

Florida Memorial College was moved to Miami.

1969

April 11. A study released by the University of Miami's Center for Advanced International Studies charged that Greater Miami's white community was not living up to its promises to improve the living conditions of the area's

Black population, and was, thereby, creating a potentially explosive situation. It also suggested white attitudes would have to change first, since Black attitudes were essentially reactions to those of the white community.

May. The January-May passenger traffic at Miami's port set a record among U.S. ports, and Miami surpassed New York City in this respect for the first time.

June. A $5,000,000 luxury terminal for cruise ships was completed, as part of the $22,000,000 Dodge Island seaport project.

The median income for Miami Blacks was $5,350, while that for Cubans was $6,550.

1970 February. By this date 182,375 Cubans had arrived on the freedom flights from Havana.

Spring. Over 364,000 Cuban exiles had registered at Miami's Cuban Refugee Center, and Cubans represented about 23 per cent of Dade County's population, with a community that numbered about 300,000.

May 10. Acting on a suit filed by two students, a Miami Circuit Court ordered President Stanford to resume classes at the University of Miami. He had closed the school in the face of anti-war protests.

June 15. Sporadic violence flared up in the city's Black sections. The incidents were sparked by the alleged sale of rotten meat to Black customers by a white-owned supermarket.

June 16. Looting, arson and sniper fire spread through the Liberty City, Brownsville and Coconut Grove Black districts during the second consecutive night of disorders. Two Blacks and two whites were wounded in separate incidents.

June 17. The rioting continued through a fourth day and night.

June 18. Relative calm was restored in the riot areas thanks to an agreement whereby City and County leaders withdrew riot control forces from the riot areas, and Black volunteers patrolled the communities. Much of the credit for the agreement went to Black City Commissioner Athalie Range.

June 19. The volunteer patrols continued their operations as calm was now restored. The four days of violence had produced several injuries but no deaths.

July 1. The National Bicentennial Commission recommended Miami as one of the sites for a multi-city celebration in 1976. The other cities were Washington, D.C., Boston, and Philadelphia.

August 8. Miami's unofficial black Mayor T. Willard Fair, resigned and urged the black community to stop the patronizing practice of selecting titular but powerless officials. He had been selected in a six-week write-in vote sponsored by the Miami Times.

Metropolitan Miami-Dade County's population was 1,267,792.

The Port of Miami's passenger volume was 569,000.

1971   April. A survey revealed that Miami was rapidly becoming "Latinized," because of the influx of more than 300,000 Cuban refugees.

April 10. Police Chief Bernard L. Garmire proposed a major reorganization of the city's police department with greater emphasis being placed on the social functions of the force.

Auguts 14. Mayor David Kennedy was easily reelected.

November 16. Fifteen Miami Negro policemen filed suit in the Federal District Court in the city, charging that Miami authorities practiced racial discrimination in the hiring and promotion of Negro policemen.

1972   January 16. The Dallas Cowboys defeated the Miami Dolphis football team in the Super Bowl, 24-3.

July. A massive voter registration drive began in the city to register Cuban-Americans. A report revealed that only one-half of the eligible 80,000 Cuban citizens in Miami had registered to vote.

July. The Democratic National Nominating Convention was held in Miami Beach.

July 6. M. Reboso, a 38 year old Cuban architect, was appointed to the Miami City Commission. He became the first Cuban exile to hold a seat on the Commission.

August. The Republican National Nominating Convention was held in Miami Beach.

November. The Miami Hotel Owners Association announced that the city spent $1,750,000 annually to promote tourism.

1973   January 14. The Miami Dolphins defeated the Washington Redskins in the Super Bowl by a score of 14-7.

February 5. A Special Florida Prosecutor, S. Boyles, began an inquiry into allegations of widespread corruption in the courts and local governments of Miami and Dade County.

February 17. The inquiry into alleged corruption in Miami and Dade County was halted temporarily by legal action taken at Tallahassee.

March 14. Federal District Judge J. Eaton dismissed the petition to stop the investigation into corruption in Miami and Dade County.

April 6. Mayor Kennedy along with two judges and three other Miamians were indicted for alleged corruption and bribery. Kennedy asked to be relieved of his mayoral duties until the case was disposed of in the courts.

August 14. Although Mayor Kennedy was cleared of all charges, several other Miamians were found guilty.

November 6. Maurice A. Ferre, a Puerto Rican, was elected Mayor of Miami, indicating the political clout of the Latin community in the city.

1974   The Miami River was substantially improved

after a three year voluntary clean-up campaign. It was reported that twenty-two species of marine life had returned to the river, and that residential construction as well as recreational facility building was progressing rapidly along the banks of the river.

The city's smoldering economic problems were compounded further by the energy shortage that disrupted tourism, the city's major industry.

1975

March. A Miami Census revealed that Cubans comprised 52 per cent of Miami's inner city population.

June. More than 200,000 Latin visitors, mainly from South America, arrived in the city, thereby improving the prospects for the summer tourist season.

September 25. Miami attempted to avoid a Federal Law Suit and possible loss of $10 million in Federal funds by beginning a program to end discrimination in hiring practices for municipal and Federally financed jobs.

November 4. Mayor Maurice Ferre was easily reelected.

December 3. Four bombs exploded outside buildings that housed Federal offices in Miami. Anti-Castro Cuban exiles were suspected.

December 4. Several bombs exploded on the second floor of Miami Police Headquarters. Again Anti-Castro Cubans were blamed for the bombings.

December 14. By this date, nine bombings had taken place in Miami over a ten day period. A group calling itself Jin claimed responsibility for this outbreak of violence, and Anti-Cuban sentiment began to grow stronger in the city.

1976

A Federal Grand Jury that had been investigating an IRS project called Operation Leprechaun, a scheme that reportedly included gathering information on the sexual and drinking activities of Federal and local officials in the Miami area, resumed work after questioning IRS Commissioner Donald C. Alexander.

The Cuban Community in Miami had increased to nearly 400,000 residents.

DOCUMENTS

Selecting fewer than one hundred pages of documents to highlight the history of a major metropolitan center is a difficult and highly subjective task. Aside from the paucity of material on the 1930-50 period, an attempt has been made to present a chronologically balanced selection that touches on the major trends and events in Miami's history. Hopefully, the selections illustrate the city's multi-facted character and indicate the variety of sources available for studying it.

A SPANIARD MAROONED IN DADE COUNTY
1575

The first recorded white man to reside in the area of present-day Dade County was Hernando d'Escalante Fontaneda. Fontaneda was shipwrecked off the Florida coast when he was 13 years old, probably in 1545, and he spent the next 17 years as a captive of the Tequesta Indians, a branch of the Calusa Federation under Chief Carlos. Though a virtual slave, he was permitted to traverse the territory controlled by the Federation. The following excerpts from his _Memoir_ (c. 1575) describe the Indians of the Florida Keys and the South Florida region, and the interpreter's role he played for other captured Spaniards.

Source: Hernando d'Escalante Fontaneda, _Memoir of Do d'Escalante Fontaneda Respecting Florida_, translated with notes by Buckingham Smith, reprinted with revisions (Miami: University of Miami and Historical Association of Southern Florida, 1944), 11-14, 19-20.

There are yet other islands, nearer to the mainland, stretching between the west and east, called the Martires; for the reason that many men have suffered on them, and also because certain rocks rise there from beneath the sea, which, at a distance, look like men in distress. Indians are on these islands, who are of a large size: the women are well proportioned, and have good countenances. On these islands there are two Indian towns; in one of them the one town is called Guarugunbe, which in Spanish is _pueblo de Llanto_, the town of weeping; the name of the other little town, Cuchiyaga, means the place where there has been suffering.

These Indians have no gold, less silver, and less clothing. They go naked, except only some breech-cloths woven of palm, with which the men cover themselves; the women do the like with certain grass that grows on trees. This grass looks like wool, although it is different from it.

The common food is fish, turtle, and snails (all of which are alike fish), and tunny and whale; which is according to what I saw while I was among these Indians. Some eat sea-wolves; not all of them, for there is a distinction between the higher and the lower classes, but the principal persons eat them. There is another fish which we here call <u>langosta</u> (lobster), and one like unto a <u>chapin</u> (trunkfish), of which they consume not less than of the former.

On these islands are many deer, and a certain animal that looks like a fox, yet is not, but a different thing from it. It is fat and good to eat. On other islands are very large bears; and, as the islands run from west to east, and the land of Florida passes eastwardly towards these islands that must be the reason of bears being on them; for the mainland is near, and they can cross from island to island. But what was a great wonder to the captives who were there, and to those of us in other places, was the existence of deer on the Islands of Cuchiyaga, the town of which I have spoken. Much more would I relate of each thing, but that I have other objects which concern me more, and I leave it.

On these islands is likewise a wood we call here <u>el palo para muchas cosas</u> (the wood for many uses), well known to physicians; also much fruit of many sorts, which I will not enumerate. as, were I to attempt to do so, I should never finish.

To the west of these islands is a great channel, which no pilot dares go through with a large vessel; because, as I have said, of some islands that are on the opposite side towards the west, which are without trees, and formed of sand. . . .

Running from south to north between Habana and Florida, the distance to the Tortugas and the Martires is forty leagues; twenty leagues to the Martires, and thence other twenty to Florida--to the territory of Carlos, a province of Indians, which in their language signifies, a fierce people, they are so-called for being brave and skillful, as in truth they are. They are masters of a large district of country, as far as a town they call Guacata, on the Lake of Mayaimi /Lake Okeechobee/ which is called Mayaimi because it is very large. Around it are many little villages, which I will speak about hereafter. The distance in going from Habana to the farthest islands, which are beyond the Cape of the Martires and almost adjoin Florida, is sixty leagues; because those islands are near seventy leagues in extent, and run from west to east.

This channel has many passages, and many different outlets and little channels. The principal channel is very wide; across it are the Islands of Vermuda, of which I have some recollection of what the Indians said; but not wishing to extend this account in that direction, I return to what I was talking about, the termination of the islands of the Martires.

Toward the north the Martires end near a place of the Indians called Tequesta, situate on the bank of a river which extends into the country the distance of fifteen leagues, and issues from another lake of fresh water, which is said by some Indians who have traversed it more than I, to be an arm of the Lake of Mayaimi. On this lake of fresh water, which lies in the midst of the country, are many towns, of thirty or forty inhabitants each; and as many more places there are in which people are not so numerous. They have bread of roots, which is their common food the greater part of the time; and because of the lake, which rises in some seasons so high that the roots cannot be reached in consequence of the water, they are for some time without eating this bread. Fish is plenty and very good. There is another root, like the truffle over here, which is sweet; and there are other different roots of many kinds; but when there is hunting, either deer or birds, they prefer to eat meat or fowl. I will also mention, that in the rivers of fresh water are infinite quantities of eels, very savory, and enormous trout. The eels are nearly the size of a man, thick as the thigh, and some of them are smaller. The Indians also eat lagartos (alligators), and tortoises /opossum/, and many more disgusting reptiles which, if we were to continue enumerating, we should never be through.

These Indians occupy a very rocky and a very marshy country. They have no product of mines, or thing that we have in this part of the world. The men go naked, and the women in a shawl made of a kind of palm-leaf, split and woven. They are subjects of Carlos, and pay him tribute of all the things I have before mentioned, food and roots, the skins of deer, and other articles. . . .

As he was newly captured, or found, and understood not the Indians, I and Juan Rodriguez were the interpreters for this man, and others, as wel already knew the language. It was a consolation, though a sad one, for those who were lost after us to find on shore Christian companions who could share their hardships and help them to understand those brutes. Many Spaniards have saved their lives by finding themselves with Christian companions already there. For the natives who took them would order them to dance and sing; and as they did not understand, and the Indians themselves are very mean, (for the most so of any are the people of Florida,) they thought the Christians were rebellious, and unwilling to do so. And so they would kill them, and report to their cacique that for their meanness and rebelliousness they had been slain, because they would not do as they were told; which was the answer, as I have said, made to the cacique when he would ask why they had killed them. One day, I, a negro, and two others, Spaniards recently made captives, being present, the cacique, in conversation with his vassals and the great chiefs of his train about what I have just mentioned, asked me, I being mas ladino (better acquainted with the language than any one), saying: "Escalante, tell us the truth, for you well know that I like you much: When we tell these, your companions, to dance and sing, and do other things, why are they so mean and rebellious that they will not? cr is it that they do not fear death, or will not yield to a people unlike them in their religion? Answer me; and if you do not know the reason, ask it of those newly seized, who for their own fault are captives now, a people whom once we held to be gods come down from the sky." And I, answering my lord and master, told him the truth: "My Lord, as I understand it, they are not contrary, nor is it for any evil reason, but it is because they cannot understand you, which they earnestly strive to do." He said it was not true; that often he would command them to do things, and sometimes they would obey him, and at others they would not, however much they might be told. I said to him: "Even so, my lord, they do not intentionally behave amiss, nor for perversity, but from not understanding. Speak to them, that I may be a witness, and likewise this your free negro." And the cacique laughingly, said: "Se-le-te-ga," to the new comers; and they asked what it was he said to them. The negro, who was near to them, laughed, and said to the cacique: "Master, I will tell you the truth; they have not understood, and they ask Escalante what it is you say, and he does not wish to tell them until you command him.: Then the cacique believed the truth, and said to me: "Declare it to them, Escalante; for now do I really believe you." I made known to them the maening of Se-le-tega, which which is, "Run to the look-out, see if there be any people coming;" they of Florida abbreviate their words more than we. The cacique, discovering the truth, said to his vassals, that when they should find Christians thus cast away, and seize them, they must require them to do nothing without giving notice, that one might go to them who should understand their language.

EXPANSION BRINGS INCORPORATION
1896

With the extension of Henry Flagler's Florida East Coast Railroad to Miami in 1896, the quiet riverside community expanded rapidly. From less than 500 residents at the beginning of 1896, Miami's population rose to about 1,500 by midyear. On July 28, the town's 343 voters (some sources place the figure at 502), acted under the state's general municipal incorporation law and approved the incorporation of the City of Miami. John Reilly was chosen mayor, and seven councilmen were selected along with other municipal officers. The following article from the first issue of Miami's first newspaper, the Miami Metropolis, summarizes why incorporation was an urgent matter in July 1896.

Source: Miami Metropolis, May 15, 1896, reprinted in John Sewell, John Sewell's Memoirs and History of Miami, Florida (Miami?: Franklin Press, 1933), 94-95.

INCORPORATE AT ONCE

We should take steps to incorporate the town of Miami without delay. There will be 1,500 people before the 1st of July and while the absence of saloons has a great deal to do with insuring the peace of the town, still it is necessary to incorporate and organize a good, strong municipal government as soon as possible.

The steps should be taken carefully. It should not be left to the haphazard judgment of the man, or men, upon whom the drawing up of an advertisement of notice of incorporation should fall, to exercise his own sweet will as to the location of the town boundaries and the amount of territory the municipality should embrace. We ought to incorporate so as to be able to frame and enforce such ordinances as are necessary.

Sanitary matters should be looked after. The removal of excrement and all kinds of disease-producing products at stated intervals should be rigidly insisted upon. No use to put clauses in the contracts and deeds to insure a model town if nuisances can be committed in and about the business center and dead fish deposited without stint on the river shore about the city dock. An ounce of prevention in prohibiting houses of ill fame from getting a foothold is worth a ton of Parkhurstism after they are well rooted. Indecent bathing should be prohibited within the town limits and Sunday should be well observed.

For these and many other reasons the town should be incorporated before August 1st. Why not call a meeting and appoint a committee to take the matter in hand and, above all, try to get a decent set of officers for the first year? They will be more needed then than at any future time. We know that the holder of a municipal office gets little, if any pay, not much honor and an abundance of abuse. But our best business men should be willing to serve for a year or two at least, so as to get the town established on a proper basis.

POLITICS AND MERRYMAKING
1907

Miami's pioneers took their politics seriously, but they were not averse to spicing political campaigns with considerable merrymaking. Elections became social as well as political events, and Miamians thoroughly enjoyed themselves while conduting the business at hand. The following account of part of the 1907 local election testifies to this singular talent for combining politics and entertainment.

Source: Isidor Cohen, Historical Sketches and Sidelights of Miami, Florida (Miami: private printing, 1925), 52-56, 30-32, 56-57.

The agitation for deep water in Miami Harbor was then at its height. In order to commit the numerous candidates aspiring for office to the deep-water project, its proponents called a mass meeting which every candidate had pledged to attend, and did attend. The auditorium was crowded beyond its capacity, and as the clock struck 8 P.M. things commenced to happen in rapid succession. In the midst of a tense silence, Judge Frank B. Stoneman (then editor of the Miami *Record*) arose from his seat in the rear of the hall and in stentorian tones declaimed, "In view of the fact that the appointed time for the opening of this meeting has passed, I move to adjourn." This unexpected motion received a spontaneous and unanimous second from all candidates present (the candidates were eager to escape the ordeal of speech-making). A motion to adjourn being undebatable..., the large audience maintained an ominous silence until it was submitted for voting, when it was shouted down in a thunderous "no" that shook the flimsy walls of the building. The disposition of this sensational motion was followed by loud and persistent calls of names of prominent citizens in the audience to act as chairman of the meeting. The name uttered the loudest happened to be that of E. A. Waddel, who made his first appearance at a public meeting.

Mr. Waddel met this call by feigning illness and pleading to be excused. His refusal to preside, however, was interpreted by the audience as pure modesty, for which he has always been noted, and was therefore unheeded. Thereupon H. M. King, the undertaker, advanced toward the victim of circumstances at a professional gait and seizing the former by the lapels of his coat, attempted to drag him to the platform. After considerable struggle that ceased on the victim's realization of the futility of resisting an undertaker, he allowed himself to be escorted to the platform, where he remained standing for some time scrutinizing the agitated audience. At last, pointing an accusing finger in the writer's direction, he shouted, "You are the one that's responsible for this confounded meeting. . ., come over here and preside."

At this stage of the proceedings the audience, being thoroughly imbued with the spirit of the occasion, burst out in a campaign song which ended with the refrain, "What's the matter with Waddel? He is alright." Upon restoration of order, the writer yielded to the good-natured demand to preside and assumed charge of the spirited meeting in the course of which some remarkable speeches were delivered by the candidates that dared remain in the hall. Deep water for Miami Harbor was the keynote of every discourse inflicted upon the long-suffering audience that night, ...

The first speaker, John W. Watson, who was a candidate for the legislature, in a forceful speech, reviewed his past official record and pledged his support to the deep-water project. G. A. Worley, the former's opponent, pleaded that he would not only push the deepening of Miami Harbor with all the force at his command, but would in defiance of the Florida East Coast Railway Corporation partisans cut down the wire fence which was put up along the bay shore, between Flagler Street and the terminal dock, by the Florida East Coast Railway Corporation. . . .

W. W. Prout . . . started his harrangue with a vitriolic attack upon the railway corporation accusing it of trying to ruin Miami by building the oversea railroad to Key West, and finished with the inevitable deep-water climax. Frank Wharton, Mr. Prout's opponent for the mayoralty, and the rest of the candidates, after taking an oath of allegiance to the deep-water project, in tones that were calculated not to lose them any votes, recited their genealogies for the delectation and instruction of their highly appreciative audience. Some of them modestly claimed direct descent from the feudal barons of Scotland, from Captain Kidd, the pirate, and one of the candidates, a more adroit politician than the rest, claimed descent from the lost tribes of Israel--the last, of course, was a bid for the chairman's vote. At a little past midnight, a motion to adjourn by some one in the audience, whose brain was still functioning, put an end to what was threatened to be an all-night session. . . .
The contest /a baseball game held as part of the campaign/ "the contest proved all it was expected to be, sensational from start to finish. In the last inning most of the spectators took a hand, some helping the exhausted players to their bases, and others trying to kill the umpire.
The two most exciting features of that historic game were: a most wonderful slide for the home plate by County Clerk Z. T. Merritt (avoirdupois, 275 pounds), who had remained mo-

tionless within about ten feet from his goal, where he rested until the end of the game by permission of the sympathetic unpire, who announced his brilliant performance "safe," and Judge G. A. Worley's remarkable performance, a description of which follows.

All the bases were filled by players and spectators when the Judge went to bat. After bowing to the grand stand and shouting to those who admiringly surrounded him to disperse, he rubbed his hands with sand, took hold of a giant bat and looked dreamily toward the Atlantic across the bay. The spectators were awe-stricken by his dramatic pose, but soon recovered and as with one voice shouted "Judge, give 'em hell." The Judge was visibly moved by this demonstration of confidence. Standing erect in his size sixty-six blue-jeans, he looked for all the world like the famous actor DeWolf Hopper, in his role "Casey at the Bat." Like his prototype, he treated the first two balls with scorn and swung with all his might against the third, which unlike Casey, he struck full in the face and sent it flying across Biscayne Bay. This phenomenal performance was followed by a spontaneous explosion from the band that played several popular airs while the players and spectators walked, some arm in arm, around the bases to the home-plate where all joined in an ovation to the modern Casey.

. . .

The last act of that memorable campaign was staged at the city hall a few days later, when the official score-keeper handed the baseball score to the election clerk who, on finding that Frank Wharton's team had defeated Prout's by a score of twenty-seven to twenty, calmly announced that the count of the ballots (by some strange coincidence) showed a majority of seven votes in favor of Mr. Wharton. Mr. Prout, in his congratulatory remarks to his successful opponent, admitted that the election was won fair and square. However, he was distressed by his discovery that he had been credited with at least two hundred votes less than his records of pre-election promises indicated. This discrepancy led him to the conclusion that there were at least two hundred liars in the city of Miami at that time. . . .

THE COMMISSION-MANAGER PLAN FOR MIAMI
1921

In 1921 Miami joined the nearly 300 American cities that had already adopted the commission-manager formula for municipal government. In Miami, as elsewhere, this formula's attractiveness lay partially in its promise of more honest, efficient, and economical government. In addition, the new form of government enjoyed the support of Miami's business and professional elements who felt it would be more responsive to their needs. The 1921 Charter contained provisions for initiative, referendum, and recall, all popular innovations in early 20th century municipal charters because they (1) provided at least the illusion of direct democracy, and/or (2) appeased those dissatisfied with the citywide election of councilmen under commission government. Some selections from the Charter appear below.

Source: <u>Charter of the City of Miami, Florida</u>, 1921, 6-8, 16-17.

SECTION 3.
ENUMERATING THE COMMISSION'S POWERS.

(ii) To establish and set apart in said city separate residential limits or districts for white and negro residents; to designate, establish and set apart the territorial limits or districts of said city within which white persons may reside, and separate territorial limits or districts of said city within which negroes may reside; to prohibit any white person from taking up or establishing a place of residence or business within the territorial limits of said city so set apart and established for the residence of negroes, and to prohibit any negro from taking up or establishing a place or residence or business within the territorial limits of said city so set apart and established for the residence of white persons; to define the terms "resident," "residence," and "place of residence," and "business" and "place of business."

SECTION 4.

(a) General Description: The form of government of the City of Miami, Florida, provided for under this Charter shall be known as the "Commission-Manager Plan," and the Commission shall consist of five (5) citizens, who are qualified voters of the City and who shall be elected at large in manner hereinafter provided. The commission shall constitute the governing body with powers (as hereinafter provided) to pass ordinances, adopt regulations, and appoint a chief administrative officer to be known as the "City Manager," and exercise all powers conferred upon the City except as hereinafter provided.

* * *

SECTION 5.
THE INITIATIVE.
(a) POWER TO INITIATE ORDINANCES.

The people shall have power at their option to propose ordinances, including ordinances, granting franchises or privileges and to adopt the same at the polls, such power being known as the initiative. A petition, meeting the requirements hereinafter provided and requesting the commission to pass an ordinance, therein set forth or designated, shall be termed an initiative petition and shall be acted upon as hereinafter provided. . . .

(c) FILING OF PETITIONS.

Within ten days after the filing of the petition the clerk shall ascertain by examination the number of registered voters whose signatures are appended thereto and whether this number is at least ten per cent (10%) of the total number of registered voters as shown by the city registration books, and he shall attach to said petition his certificate showing the result of said examination. If, by the clerk's certificate, of which notice in writing shall be given to one or more of the persons designated, the petition is shown to be insufficient it may be amended within ten (10) days from the date of said certificate by filing supplementary petition papers with additional signatures. The clerk shall within ten (10) days after such amendment make examination of the amended petition, and if his certificate shall show the same to be insufficient, the clerk shall file the petition in his office and shall notify each member of the committee of the fact. The final finding of the insufficiency of a petition shall not prejudice the filing of a new petition for the same purpose.

(d) SUBMISSION OF PETITION TO COMMISSION.

If the petition shall be found to be sufficient, the clerk shall so certify and submit the proposed measure to the commission at its next meeting. Upon receiving the proposed measure the commission shall at once proceed to consider it and shall take final action thereon within thirty (30) days from the date it is filed with them.

(e) ELECTION ON INITIATED MEASURES.

If the commission shall fail to pass the proposed measure, or shall pass it in a form different from that set forth in the petition, then the measure shall be submitted by the commission to the vote of the electors at the next election occurring not less than thirty (30) days after the date of the final action by the commission, and if no election is to be held within six (6) months from such date, then the commission shall call a special election to be held not less than thirty (30) nor more than forty-five (45) days from such date. When submitted the measure shall be in its original form. . . .

SECTION 15.
CITY MANAGER.

The Commission shall within thirty (30) days after taking office appoint a City Manager who shall be the administrative head of the municipal government and shall be responsible for the efficient administration of all departments and may be the head of such department as the commission may by ordinance provide. He shall be chosen on the basis of his executive and administrative qualifications. He may or may not be a resident of the City of Miami or the State of Florida. No memner of the City Commission shall be appointed City Manager. He shall hold office at the will of the commission. He shall receive such salary as may be fixed by the commission.

SECTION 16.

The powers and duties of the City manager shall be:

(a) To see that the laws and ordinances are enforced.

(b) To appoint and remove, except as herein provided, all directors of the departments and all subordinate officers and employees in the departments in both the classified and unclassified service; all appointments to be upon merit and fitness alone, and in the classified service all appointments and removals to be subject to the civil service provisions of this charter.

(c) To exercise control over all departments and divisions created herein or that may be hereafter created by the commission.

(d) To attend all meetings of the commission with the right to take part in the discussion but having no vote;

(e) To recommend to the commission for adoption such measures as he may deem necessary or expedient;

(f) To keep the commission fully advised as to the financial condition and needs of the city; and

(g) To perform such other duties as may be prescribed by this charter or be required of him by ordinance or resolution of the commission.

THE BANKERS' TICKET
1921

Miami's case offers convincing evidence for those who argue that municipal reform during the Progressive Era served the interests and therefore enjoyed the support of large business groups. The city's leading businessmen and bankers were in the forefront of the campaign to adopt the commission-manager form of government. It was primarily representatives of that group who drafted the 1921 Charter, and the first five commissioners were five of Miami's most prominent bankers. Printed below is a campaign article written in support of the "bankers' ticket." It suggests why some felt financiers were particularly qualified to direct Miami's fortunes in 1921. Isidor Cohen, the article's author, was a long-time Miami merchant and a member of the committee which drafted the 1921 charter.

Source: Isidor Cohen, <u>Historical Sketches and Sidelights of Miami, Florida</u> (Miami: private printing, 1925), 191-193.

The opponents of the bankers' ticket, which has the whole-hearted support of the framers of Miami's new charter, are trying to prevent a fair test of its operation by the injection of propaganda in this campaign, the following of which are samples: "S. Bobo Dean (then editor of the Miami <u>Metropolis</u>) is attempting selfishly to gain political power through the operation of his political machine." "The newspapers have always been on opposite sides, but they are now united in their support of the bankers' ticket." "Romfh and Gilman were common bookkeepers, Lummus kept a grocery store, Leffler was an oil agent and Wilson a fish dealer." "The promotion of the bankers' ticket is an attempt at class legislation and an arrayment of capital against labor." "The bankers were put on the ticket after it was found that nobody else would run."

S. Bobo Dean is not a candidate for office. However, for the information of the many new settlers in this city I state without fear of contradiction that instead of S. Bobo Dean being a political machine builder he has proven to be a political machine wrecker. His aggressive newspaper has destroyed the most powerful political machine in the history of Dade County--the strongly organized partisans of the Florida East Coast Railway Corporation.

It is indeed very fortunate for our city to have both of its newspapers united in the present movement for a better municipal government. This is strong proof that the candidates whose election they advocate are better qualified, by virtue of their intensive training as financiers, to serve our community than those opposing them.

. . .

The fact that common bookkeepers, a grocer, an oil agent and a fish dealer have attained their present distinguished positions as heads of our leading banking institutions is sufficient proof that they are capable of successfully administering the affairs of our municipality. With due respect to their opponents and detractors, I cannot conceive of any other group of our citizens under whose guardianship we could place the **destiny** of our city with a greater degree of safety than the group composing the bankers' ticket. In addition to their professional fitness for the positions of city commissioners they are large taxpayers and are the custodians of big enterprises, which are more sensitive to municipal mismanagement than any other business. Their prestige as bankers will exercise a more beneficial influence upon the administration of our future city manager than that of men in other occupations.

I cannot conceive of any other group of our citizenship who are less likely to favor an arrayment of capital against labor or to foster strife and contentions of any kind in our community. Why, the success of our banks more than that of any other business depends upon a mutual satisfactory adjustment between the two forces. This applies with equal force to the permanent prosperity of our laboring classes. Nothing is more timid than capital. The banishment of confidence from a locality is immediately followed by a withdrawal of capital--and the results are unemployment and general depression.

The supporters of the bankers' ticket are absolutely opposed to raising a "labor and capital" issue in this campaign. Should this be forced upon them by the so-called friends of labor our people will be driven into a political alignment which will prove decidedly disadvantageous to organized labor. There is no other issue in this campaign than the issue of saving our city from economic retrogression.

Why prate of class legislation, or capital against labor? One of these praters uttered a sensible remark when he stated that this city needs an "honest-to-God non-political administration." The framers of the new charter had such an administration in view when the initiated the successful movement for a change in the fundamental principle of our municipal government. They also had this in view when they considered the qualifications of possible candidates, including the one who now decries the fostering of class rule in Miami. After careful consideration in which they were guided by the sound direction of a large number of Miami's leading business and professional men, they wisely selected the presidents of the city's five leading banking institutions, not only as "an honest-to-God non-political" aggregation, but as the logical candidates who if elected, will render the commission-manager form of government in Miami eminently successful.

The opposition candidates seem to be fond of platforms. They criticize the bankers, who have been drafted into this campaign, for their omission to compare platforms with them. Every intelligent voter is familiar with the bankers' platform without hearing it shouted at public meetings. Their platform can be summarized in two words, namely: PROGRESSIVE ADMINISTRATION. This includes an improved water system, extension of gas service, parks and playgrounds, municipal hospitals and everything else that may contribute to the happiness and prosperity of our community. . . .

BOOM TIME IN MIAMI
1925

Amidst the daily diet of "spectaculars" foisted on the American public in the 1920's, none had more impact on Miamians than the Great Florida Land Boom. In and about Miami, land prices started to rise as early as 1923, peaked in 1925, and began to drop disastrously in 1926. Along with irrational rises in real estate values, the Boom produced an aura and psychology more appropriate for a 19th century mining town than a 20th century urban center. What follows is Theyre Weigall's account of his initial encounter with Miami in August 1925. Weigall, an English journalist, remained in Miami for the rest of 1925, became a publicity writer for Coral Gables, and was thoroughly swept up by the spirit of the times.

Source: Theyre H. Weigall, Boom in Paradise (New York: Alfred H. King, 1932), 30-31, 45-48.

I leaned out of the window; and there, a few hundred yards ahead and waiting for us, was the immense crowd that was always waiting for those car-loads of gullible northerners that were disgorged every few hours into Miami Central Station. As we drew in, they swarmed around the carriages like a hive of angry bees; most of them shouting, all of them sweating, all of them coatless and carrying great bundles of papers. All the men were wearing cotton knee-breeches, and all were purple in the face with heat and excitement. There were no women. The scene, so utterly unlike Palm Beach of a few hours previously, was far more what I had anticipated of the Florida boom, but also in some subtle way infinitely more repulsive and less romantic. . . .

There are not very many taxis in Miami, but such as there are can usually be discovered somewhere in the neighbourhood of the station, and I was lucky enough to get one of them. As a matter of fact, as everyone who is able to afford to travel on wheels possess at least one car of his own, there is not a great deal of necessity of them. . . .

Within ten yards from the station we became embedded in a jam of traffic which would have made the worst congestion of London or New York child's play by comparison.

Everything was completely immovable. Even on stepping out of the train, my ears had been assailed by a peculiar din whose source I could not definitely place, but its cause soon became evident. It is, or was, the custom in Miami for any driver of any vehicle which is held up for more than a few seconds to press his finger on his electric warning signal and keep it there, as a sort of general protest against the conditions and an advertisement of the fact that he is there, and wants to get about his business. The mass effect of several hundreds of people all doing this simultaneously in a street already narrow and noisy enough, in all conscience, can better be imagined than described. The din was quite deafening, and it was not for at least ten minutes that we were able to move so much as a single foot. When for a second the jam in front of us loosened, my driver dashed forward with a loud shout into the middle of the melée, and at once collided, very violently, with a Ford-load of fat men immediately ahead. I was jolted heavily forward against the rear screen, and in the same instant saw that we had ripped part of the Ford's near-side mudguard right off its supports and badly damaged our own. To my amazement, nothing whatever happened along the lines of the usual scene that would have resulted anywhere else, even in America. The four fat business men, who had been badly jolted, turned round as one and expressed their views on the situation in singularly unpleasant language. The only remark I actually heard was from one of the rear passengers, who volunteered that he would tell the world (which he did) that my driver was a ------------------. My own driver, with many embellishments, remarked that he'd say this was no place for --------- funerals; but to my astonishment nobody got out, or even attempted to ascertain the extent of the really quite considerable damage. A second later another gap in the traffic had presented itself, and the Ford, with a violent jerk, had crashed into it and collided with somebody else further in front and started a fresh argument. My own Jehu apparently thought no further of the matter, and never even glanced at the remains of his own front mudguard, which was scarcely what it had been a few seconds ago. As a matter of fact, by the time I had been in Florida for a few days I had become quite used to these collisions, which were so constant and so unavoidable in the existing state of the traffic that unless the vehicles concerned were actually incapable of going on with their journeys nobody troubled about them at all. And a new car could always be had for the asking, anyway.

Though commonplace enough in the light of later experience, that first journey of mine from the station to the hotel seemed to me then an epic of adventure and mighty peril. After our encounter with the Ford we were again jammed for several minutes, with the deadening din of the sirens going on all round us as before; until, in fact, a sort of lighthouse tower just behind us suddenly emitted a piercing ringing sound like a demented electric bell and displayed a cryptic series of red, yellow and green lights. The driver jammed in his gears, and we all surged slowly forwards, with a good deal of bumping and shouting. A man suddenly appeared on the footboard, and with a genial smile thrust towards me a small sample-case containing a number of different coloured silk socks. I smiled deprecatingly, and waved him away; which, being apparently far less violent treatment than he was accustomed to receive, was sufficient inducement for him to open the door and come right inside.

"I haven't any money!" I bawled at him, above the din.
"They're only two dollars!" said the man. "A knockout! Look at the texture, sir--I'll tell the world it's the bee's knees!" And so, I have no doubt, it was. "I haven;t any money!" I bawled again; and then, seeing that this was treatment obviously far too mild, I altered my tone and shouted "Get out!" and gave him a shove in the direction of the door. The man made some menacing remark which I couldn't hear, and pushed the sample-case directly under my nose. Suddenly I was furious with him, and saw red. The car, at the moment, was moving slowly through the crowd; but I jerked open the door and with a sudden heave ejected him and his sample-case out into the road. He hung on to the footboard for a moment, shouting and waving his case at me; but I shut the door, and a second later he had jumped off and with a sudden seraphic smile that quite bewildered me had boarded another car going in the opposite direction. . . .

SELLING PARADISE
1925

Advertising played a crucial role as Miami's Boom snowballed. In newspapers and other literature across the nation, the glories of the new paradise were extolled by publicity writers who tended to place more confidence in their imaginations than in their facts. Theyre Weigall, who wrote promotional copy for George Merrick's Coral Gables development, describes some of the advertising activities of one of the most successful real estate ventures of the period.

Source: Theyre H. Weigall, <u>Boom in Paradise</u> (New York: Alfred H. King, 1932), 130-134, 136.

The Publicity Department of Coral Gables had an extraordinary number of ramifications, and under the guidance of Mr. J. P. Yoder, who possessed an uncanny genius for this sort of thing, masses of literature were issued from the office every day to every corner of the United States. But the organization of the Advertising Department. . . was in some respects even more remarkable still. It is an actual fact that for two years this department alone cost the Coral Gables Corporation no less than two million dollars a year, and the Publicity Department very nearly as much again. . . .

The main feature of the Advertising Department was a vast battery of electric duplicating machines, with double crews working in three eight-hour shifts all through the twenty-four hours. These machines consisted in mechanically-driven typewriters worked somewhat on the pianola principle; a slotted sheet representing a "standard sales letter" was placed on a roller, a switch was turned, and the letter was typed off at such a speed that it was actually impossible to see the keys moving with the naked eye. I believe I am correct in saying that an ordinary single-page letter could be typed in this way in fifteen seconds, and all the operator had to do was to fill in the name and address of the recipient at the top of the sheet. Each letter was thus an original copy, and was in no sense a circular. To me this Niagara of propaganda, most of it extremely subtle and indirect, had about it something that was almost terrifying. The installation itself made a noise like a distant flight of aeroplanes; an uncanny sound, and one that echoed queerly from the lighted windows of the Advertising Building in the dead hours before dawn.

I learned a good deal of American advertising methods during this period. but to the end I still found it difficult to credit that the psychology of the American public could be so utterly different from our own. Still, I have no doubt that the department knew its business a great deal better that I did, and its methods were certainly justified by results. The letters addressed to individuals were well enough, but the crudity and blatancy of many of the poster designs were past belief. The majority of these depicted an entirely mythical city, with gleaming spires and glistening domes making up an idealized blend of Moscow and Oxford, with the exception that they were invariably rising out of a tropical paradise in which lovely ladies and marvellously-dressed gallants disported themselves under the palm-trees. Advertisements of this type were by no means confined to Coral Gables; they were poured out in thousands by practically every land corporation in Florida. It is therefore scarcely necessary to add that such pictures scarcely ever bore the slightest relation to the dreary flats, occasionally intersected by a few hundred yards of white way lighting, the attractions of which they were proclaiming. Other advertisements, unillustrated, more simply proclaimed "A Steal--at 25,000 Dollars!" and left it at that; but the city of shimmering spires was the favourite. It is scarcely possible to believe that these incredible pictures could ever have been taken for even a remote resemblance to reality. One can only imagine that the average man in the street had already been trained to the habit of discounting 99 per cent of what he was told in this way, and of treating the remaining one per cent with considerable caution. . . .

Another remarkable branch of the Coral Gables Advertising Department was the free transport service, which was operated between the city and various points throughout the United States. "Prospects" were collected practically anywhere and were transported to Coral Gables entirely free of charge, afterwards being given a royal time for two or three days while they were being shown round the city as the guests of the Corporation. The transport fleet consisted of no less than seventy-six vehicles, each capable of accomodating twenty-three passengers in very considerable luxury. About twenty of these units were run on regular schedules between Coral Gables and practically all the larger cities of the southern states. Many of these regular runs extended to over five hundred miles; actually the longest was that between Coral Gables and Montgomery, Alabama, a distance of 881 miles. This journey was performed three times weekly in both directions. In addition, occasional runs were made from points as far distant as New York, Chicago, and even San Francisco, covering anything up to four thousand miles. It was not only Coral Gables that operated these services--Hollywood, Davis Islands, Boca Raton and Miami Shores, to mention only a few of its rivals, possessed fleets scarcely less large. The expense was of course colossal, but the statistics showing the resultant sales were said to prove that it was amply justified. . . .

Apart from the publicity and advertising campaigns being carried on from our own offices, we worked too in conjunction with most of the semi-public organizations that were broadcasting the delights of the Only Tropical Paradise further and yet further afield. The Chambers of Commerce, Progress Associations, Boosters, Elks, Kiwanis, Shriners, Rotarians, and every other club and order in the country was helping in the good work, and by the end of 1925 it was impossible to open a newspaper anywhere in the United States without finding some reference to Florida and Florida's activities. . . .

SYNDICATES FOR SPECULATORS
1925

Land syndicates provided a means whereby non-residents could seek their share of the fantastic profits being made in Miami and its environs. Northern newspapers carried frequent announcements concerning the formation of such syndicates. Most notices, like the first below from the New York Times, were quite uninformative. Apparently, the organizers either intended to intrigue prospective investors, or they were counting on a general public faith in the success potential of any Florida land venture to entice money into their schemes. The second advertisement, taken from the New York Sun, is unusual for the amount of detail supplied, and for the fact that it was directed at a specific group of prospective investors.

Source: (a) New York Times, September 6, 1925.
(b) New York Sun, May 9, 1925.

(a)

You Can Share in

Florida's Harvest of

Real Estate Profits

A Syndicate is now forming for the purpose of buying and selling, for profit, large blocks of property on the East Coast of Florida - principally between Miami and Palm Beach. This Syndicate is headed by one of Miami's most reputable and successful real estate operators - a man who has built many of the finest business structures, hotels, apartment houses and homes in Miami. Syndicate capital represented by Trust Certificates of $100 each. All officers of the Syndicate to be bonded to cover moneys paid in. For details, address P.J., Box 711, Times Downtown.

(b)

ADVERTISEMENT OF CLIFFORD SYNDICATE

Miami
FLORIDA

"The Land of Sunshine, Health
and Wealth"

MEN and WOMEN

of Moderate Means

Frequently believe that it is possible only for the wealthy to make profits in Miami -- this impression is incorrect

The Clifford Endowment
Realty Plan

was devised for the special purpose of making it possible for the men and women of moderate means to have an opportunity to invest as well as share in the tremendous profits to be made in Miami real estate, and at the same time be guaranteed against the loss of the purchase price, which you pay not to us, but to the

TRUST COMPANY
OF NORTH AMERICA

who in turn issues to you a certificate of deposit in your name calling for the payment of same to you in CASH at a future date. So when you get your deed you also obtain from the Trust Company THE FULL AMOUNT OF YOUR PURCHASE PRICE IN CASH

<u>According to the Terms of Your Contract, in case of Death Your Heirs get Deed to the Property without further payment</u>

The Clifford Endowment Realty plan means to you
SAFETY PLUS
INSURANCE
PLUS PROFITS
PLUS MONEY BACK

Write us for particulars regarding

A FREE TRIP TO
MIAMI

An enchanting ten-day trip on one of the beautiful Clyde

Line steamers to buyers of lots under the Clifford Endowment Realty Plan Contract at

SEA VIEW PARK

which is only about half a mile south of city limits of Greater Miami; three-quarters of a mile from School, also club, half a mile from railroad station and stores; on the famous Red Road, about two and a half miles from $10,000,000 Hotel; two miles from Coral Gables, a $30,000,000 development, AND COCO PLUM BEACH, the keystone of a $100,000,000 development.

An 80-foot boulevard is already under course of construction, with a 20-foot parkway in centre of same, the parkway being beautified with coconut trees and hibiscus plants. Coral rock roads are being installed and red cement sidewalks are being laid as rapidly as possible.

Only a Few Choice Sites Left
$1500 and up
Terms are Within Reach of All

CLIFFORD COUNTRY ESTATES
Inc.
565 5th Ave., New York City

THE BINDER BOYS
1925

During the Boom days of 1925, the "binder boys" were a familiar sight in and around Miami. They were the type of individuals - entrepreneurial to some, parasitical to others - who naturally gravitate to areas where speculation presents the opportunity for a "killing." Hustling deals along Flagler Street, gobbling up lots at subdivision auctions, and assaulting new arrivals at the train station, they seemed omnipresent amidst spiraling real estate values. The following selection from Kenneth Ballinger's informative work profiles the "binder boys" and describes their methods.

Source: Kenneth Ballinger, <u>Miami Millions: The Dance of the Dollars in the Great Florida Land Boom of 1925</u> (Miami: The Franklin Press, 1936), 97-99.

The "BINDER BOY" was a peculiar outcropping of the Florida boom and was evident in obnoxious numbers from March through August, 1925. At the end of that period, the binder boys began leaving Miami and other boom centers like angry bees out of a hive, many so impoverished that they were glad to get space in empty Northbound freight trains.

A composite picture of the binder boy possibly would reveal an individual slightly under normal height, never very clean or neat, bending every effort to make a lot of money in a hurry without the slightest pretense of remaining in Florida once that was done. He was attired in golf knickers, because they didn't need pressing nor the addition of a coat, and the binder boy made the knicker at one time standard male daytime garb in almost any gathering, even church.

He spoke in a peculiar dialect, which soon had even the natives pronouncing the word "binder" to rhyme with "cinder" instead of with "kinder." He slept in hotel or rooming house halls, three and four to a single room, or wherever he could find temporary space.

Headquarters in Miami for the binder boys was the Ponce de Leon Hotel, principally because it was the largest downtown commercial hotel close to the big real estate

estate offices. The binder boys never got very near the tourist hotels. . . .

By July the routine of the incoming real estate operators was stripped down to bare essentials. They alighted from the train and looked about for someone who knew his way out of the depot. "Is this Miami?" usually was the first question. Then, "Where can I rent an office?" "What is the price of acreage?" By the first of July, the city of Miami had issued 5,917 real estate brokers' licenses and was putting new ones out at the rate of 60 a day.

That was the only time that a Miami journal ever went on record as opposing the immigration of honest and law-abiding citizens. Somewhat wearily, The Herald declared, "We no longer get a thrill out of the announcement that someone is coming to Miami to engage in the real estate business. We really feel that Miami has all the real estate dealers necessary." One might as well have whistled into a gale!

The mechanics of the binder were not complex. It is the customary thing now, as then, for a person contracting to buy a lot for, say, $5,000, to put up 10 per cent or less of the agreed purchase price to seal the bargain until the necessary formalities could be gone through with to close the deal. The buyer would receive a binder receipt, and at the end of 30 days would pay possibly another 15 per cent to complete the first payment upon the transfer of the property.

But the binder boys who came here upon the heels of the abbreviated 1924-25 winter season found that binders were just as good as money. Having more native shrewdness than capital, they first began swapping binders among themselves in the crowds that overflowed into Flagler Street from the Ponce de Leon lobby. First they made small profits on the binders themselves, and then quickly worked into the business of running up the price of a lot through several transactions while the lot still was on one binder.

The movement spread like wildfire, somewhat similar to the margin speculating on the New York Stock Exchange, and for five months at least the binder boys set a pace that had the ordinary citizens glassy-eyed and breathless.

It was not unusual, real estate men declare, for a lot to change hands as many as eight times from the day when the first buyer got his binder until the deal finally was closed. When closing time came, the buyers would group around the papers like hungry boys around a picnic pie, each with his real estate man at his elbow ready to take a slice out of the profits. Usually, by trading papers, it was possible for a deed to issue only to the last buyer, but it might have seven or eight mortgages clinging to it like ticks on a cow, each representing the profit of one of the principals along the line. The real estate brokers usually got most of the actual cash involved.

The hours of the binder boy were from 9 o'clock until 2 in the afternoon, when the banks closed. Checks were rushed at once to depositories for the cash. Time was the very essence of success until midafternoon arrived, when a check became just another piece of paper.

Several highly entertaining fiction stories were printed after the boom, attempting to show that the phenomenal sale of Seminole Beach early in August was deliberately planned to drive the binder boys out of Miami Beach, and that it really broke the back of the boom. . . .

Two versions were evolved by these writers. One had it that only alternate strips of Seminole Beach were sold on the first day, and that after all the binder boys had flocked in and were hooked the parallel unsold strips were thrown on the market a few days later at greatly reduced prices, and the binder equities dissolved like snowballs in the hot place. The other version said that after Seminole Beach was sold, the same interests opened adjoining subdivisions of equal merit but much lower-priced, to destroy the value of the lots on which the binder boys had sunk their all.

Records of the times show, however, that all of Seminole Beach was sold in one day, and was resold within a few days thereafter. They also show that while two parts of Golden Beach were put on Seminole Beach, the prices were approximately the same and the volume of sales inconsiderable when other contemporaneous sales are considered. But it made good reading. . . .

The binder boy went as he came, only some left on the tie-rods and for several years thereafter contributed no little to the unfavorable attitude toward Florida that persists in some quarters of the country. It is of the binder boy that we think when we shudder gently and cry, "Deliver us from another such boom!"

DESTRUCTION RAKES MIAMI
1926

The real estate boom was exhausted by September 1926. A numbing note of finality was added by a hurricane which struck the Florida coast on September 18, 1926. It slammed into Miami at about 1:00 A.M., and after apparently abating about 7:00 A.M., it struck with renewed fury an hour later, multiplying its human and material toll. Below is an eyewitness account of the storm's impact.

Source: *New York Times*, September 21, 1926, pp. 1-2.

FORT PIERCE, Fla., Sept 20 - Kirby Jones. . . who left Miami on the first train out after the storm, described today conditions in that city during the hurricane.

"The storm started at 1 A.M. Saturday," he said, "and raged until 2 P.M. Sunday. It started with a terrific wind followed a few minutes later by heavy rains. About 7 A.M. Saturday both wind and rain abated.

"It was this lull which indirectly caused most of the casualties. Hundreds of persons believing the storm was over, started for work. But about 8 o'clock the rain began again, and the wind grew more and more violent.

"The city was covered with a pall of darkness which obscured everything. Between 9 o'clock and noon the wind velocity reached its maximum. Thousands of homes were ripped from their foundations, and the air was filled with flying timbers.

"I was in a building seeking shelter from the storm when the roof caved in. There were about 150 other people with me at the time. All of us fled to a school house a block away.

"It was a pitiful sight to see that crowd running through the driving rain, barely able to make headway against the terrific force of the wind.

Stayed in School Until Lull

"Women were crying hysterically and children whimpering that they did not want to die, their voices almost inaudible in the roar of the wind. And all the while, flying timbers and glass were falling all about us.

"We reached the school house and remained there until noon. Then the storm abated once more and three hours later stopped.

"The city was without water because mains everywhere had burst and the authorities were compelled to cut the water off.

"I saw people catching rainwater in saucepans as it dropped from the roof in order to make coffee.

"Late in the afternoon I went down town to survey the damage. Flagler Street was littered with tangled trolley and telephone wires, and almost every window in the buildings on either side shattered.

"All electrical signs had been blown down. The Meyer-Kiser Bank Building was worst hit. Every window was broken, and huge holes gaped in the walls.

"The Columbus and McAllister hotels and almost every other building along Bay Shore Drive suffered considerable damage, and sections of the roof of the Hotel Royal Palm appeared to be missing.

Autos Battered into Junk

"Bay Shore Drive was littered with the battered hulks of automobiles, many of which had been lifted clear of the street and deposited in front yards.

"Along Bay Shore Drive are numerous second-hand automobile dealers who park their cars in lots in the open. These cars were virtually ripped to pieces and the lots, strewn with fragments, resembled heaps of discarded tin cans.

"At that time no word had been received from Miami Beach, but it was reported that large sections of the old causeway had been torn away. The Venetian Causeway, however, appeared to be intact, although the authorities would not permit anyone to attempt to cross it.

"It was also reported that the tower had been ripped loose from the Fleetwood Hotel in Miami Beach and that the entire beach section was inundated with three feet of water.

"All ships in the harbor were damaged and many of them lifted high and dry and carried inland for nearly fifty yards.

"Others were sunk in Biscayne Bay and all the city piers suffered heavy damage.

"There was no home in all Miami that did not suffer some damage. Thousands were completely destroyed.

Hotels Opened to Homeless

"I believe that 300 persons were killed and 20,000 persons rendered homeless. Immediately after the storm all hotels were thrown open to the homeless, as well as all school houses and other public buildings.

"Hundreds of persons lost everything they had except the clothes that were on their backs.

"When the storm was over scores of people could be seen in bathing suits on almost any street and many were compelled to go to work in bathing suits.

"Early Sunday morning they started clearing the wreckage from the streets, but it probably will be a week before the streets are open and probably that long before the city lighting system can be put in operation again.

"It will be a month before the city can get its telephone system working again, and probably years before the houses can be rebuilt."

ASSURANCE FROM THE MAYOR
1926

Within a week of the storm, Mayor Edward C. Romfh issued the "Official Storm Statement" printed below. It is a remarkable document because while it includes statistics on storm damage and makes a qualified appeal for aid, these themes are overshadowed by comments clearly designed to emphasize the limited damage suffered by the city and the astonishingly swift recovery allegedly underway. The reason for Romfh's remarks is understandable. Tourism was Miami's lifeblood, and the hurricane struck less than two months before the new season was to open. The mayor was essentially saying that "Fun in the Sun" was still available in Miami.

Source: From the Collections of the Coconut Grove Library Association as printed in Frank B. Sessa, "Real Estate Expansion and Boom in Miami and its Environs During the 1920's" (Ph.D. dissertation, University of Pittsburgh, 1950), following p. 340.

OFFICIAL STORM STATEMENT

Mayor E. C. Romfh gives exact facts of Miami damage and tells of rapid rehabilitation city is making

"From the thousands of telegrams pouring into Miami, hundreds of which are addressed to the mayor of the city, I am convinced a very much exaggerated idea of Miami's real condition has been created. I regard it as a duty to the public at large to set forth as briefly as possible the situation as it now exists and its relation to the future of this city.

"The West Indian hurricane which swept over an area of 60 miles on the Atlantic coast on September 18, extending 30 miles north and 30 miles south of Miami, was by far the most severe and destructive storm that ever touched the mainland of the United States. Miami in her 30 years of existence has never been materially damaged before.

"There was a great amount of damage to buildings through their unroofing, the breaking of windows and the blowing down of poorly constructed buildings in the outlying districts. The larger business buildings, the better constructed homes, hotels and apartments were mostly damaged by the breaking of glass and in some instances the covering of roofs were lossened or blown off and thus the heavy rain created the most damage. There was great destruction to the tropical plants and foliage.

"The electric light plant, water and gas systems were put out of commission. The water and gas system now is normal. The electric system has been restored in the central business district and service to large residential areas is being added daily.

"The most regrettable part of the storm was the number of deaths which totals 106 to date in Dade county. There were 851 injured placed in regular and temporary hospitals, 450 of whom have been discharged. The citizens committee did heroic work the first few days in caring for the injured. However, this work has now been taken over by the Red Cross and this organization is handling the situation with the utmost efficiency.

"Small buildings in outlying districts, cheaply constructed, were blown down. It was in these and in houseboats that the greatest number of deaths occurred. There was great damage done to yachts and pleasure boats, but most of these will be put in shipshape order for the coming season.

"It is remarkable that a city of 160,000 or more people should have gone through such a severe storm with comparatively so small number of dead and injured. This is accounted for by the fact that this city has the largest percentage of concrete buildings of any city in the United States.

"Of the 150 hotels in Miami, Miami Beach and Coral Gables, 75 per cent were not damaged to any great extent. The year around hotels are operating as usual. Of the 1,200 apartment houses, 70 per cent received little damage. All hotels and apartment houses will be completely repaired and put in first class condition within 60 days.

"There are thousands who have lost all and are destitute and who must have financial aid in order to get back upon a self-supporting basis. There are the smaller home owners, smaller tradesmen, workers and people of very moderate means. It is to aid these people that the citizens relief committee and the Red Cross issue their appeal for assistance. That need is acute and genuine.

"But there are other thousands who have the finances or can make satisfactory arrangements to restore their own homes and replace effects damaged or destroyed. These are contributing to the aid of their destitute neighbors, but financing their own losses makes it impossible for them to contribute in sufficient amounts to supply all the urgent needs. Miami greatly appreciates the spontaneous sympathy which has been shown by the American people as expressed by President Coolidge.

"In the six days that have passed since the storm, this city has come back with a speed that is absolutely amazing. No one who has not been on the ground, checking up the progress, can realize the tremendous recovery a united, courageous, indefatigable citizenship has made.

"Day and night, with little sleep, tens of thousands of men and women have co-operatively labored, not only to relieve the suffering, to feed the hungry, to house the homeless, but to repair, rebuild and to remove the debris left in the wake of the storm.

"I want to give positive assurance that our friends will find Miami this winter the same enjoyable, hospitable, comfortable vacation city it has always been.

"I predict that Miami will make a world record comeback. The people here have the enthusiasm, the will to do, an unshaken faith in the future of this great city. It is the same people who have created the fastest growing city in America who are now turning their energies and enthusiasm to the work of reconstruction in Miami.

(Signed) E. C. ROMFH, Mayor.
"CITY OF MIAMI."

Sept. 24, 1926.

HUMANITARIAN VS. ECONOMIC INTERESTS
1926

Mayor Romfh was joined in his effort to reassure prospective vacationers by others who had a stake in the tourist industry. The first document below is part of a full-page advertisement placed in the *New York Times* by the Seaborne Air Line Railway under the title "THE TRUTH ABOUT STORM DAMAGE IN FLORIDA." It represents perfectly the "it's-not-really-so-bad" propaganda. This piece is followed by some remarks from the National Chairman of the Red Cross delivered at a Washington convention. Mr. Payne made clear his conviction that selfish economic interests had seriously hindered the collection of relief funds.

Source: (a) *New York Times*, October 13, 1926, p. 11.
(b) *New York Times*, October 5, 1926, p. 4.

(a)

It is regrettable that the good faith of certain public officials in Florida has been questioned by a high official of the American Red Cross because of their statements limiting the storm damage to actual conditions. There is no purpose here to detract from the admirable service performed by the American Red Cross, nor to impede its collection of funds for the storm sufferers.
It is unfortunate that calls for money for helping those in distress were not confined to the directions in which relief was required and not leave deductions to be drawn of wholesale ruin or devastation of a city or of a community.

The President of this railroad has had the opportunity to judge of the public spirit of the Governor of Florida; of the mayor and city commissioners of Miami, and of public officials of the affected localities: they have earned the confidence of the people of Florida.

Mayor Romfh of Miami and other public officials were required by the very nature of their offices to inform the public of the facts concerning the business, general condition and the future of their respective communities. This was unfairly characterized as placing "tourist business" above the proper care of those in distress.

First reports coming from the storm area were "greatly exaggerated." This was the expression used by Florida

public officials and it was properly used. . . .
In view of these conditions there was no foundation for such statements as "Miami Wiped Out," "Miami Prostrate," "Miami Destroyed," and like terms applied to other points affected. . . .

Florida--the world's winter playground--with its unmatched climate, its fertile soil which has no superior, the length of its seasons, its freedom from the rigors of winters, will continue to prosper and grow, and the area affected by this storm will take on a new aspect, profiting by the experience gained.

S. DAVIES WARFIELD
President, Seaboard Air Line Railway

(b)

The Florida situation was taken up at the day session . . . by . . . /the/ Chairman of the Red Cross, who laid aside his prepared address and protested against the activities of "officials and special interests" in Florida to minimize the losses caused by the hurricane.

Says Disaster Is Greater Than Told

"I think I ought to tell you what led to the statement I gave out last week on the Florida situation." Mr. Payne said, "I want to tell you the disaster in Florida is really much greater than the interests there would have us believe, and there is going on in Florida a conflict between the humanitarian efforts of some on the one side and the selfishness of business on the other.

"The time has come when we must consider seriously whether it is too late to renew our campaign for the relief of the poor and stricken in the storm area."

The first intimation he had of what was going on, Mr. Payne said, was when the Chairman of the Chicago chapter called him up and read a message Governor Martin had sent to Mayor Deever of Chicago, thanking him for offers of aid and assuring the Mayor, he, the Governor, would let him know if further assistance was necessary.

"At first," Mr. Payne went on, "I could scarcely believe that a Governor would be such an idiot as to make such a statement right at the height of a campaign to raise money for the relief of the poor people of his state.

"I suppose that the desire of a group to protect its business interests is a natural weakness," Mr. Payne said.

"But the poor victims of the storm are regarded as of less importance than the tourist business.

"The time has come for the American Red Cross to

speak out. There are times and circumstances when not to speak out is at least to connive. The American Red Cross can never connive in a falsehood.

"The American people should still be ready to go forward and provide adequate relief for the many people in Florida who are in dire need of it. We have something more than $3,000,000 now. What we will do in the future rests with you. Some effort should be made to complete our campaign. We should at least have the satisfaction of feeling that we have done our utmost."

THE ASSASSIN'S BULLET
1933

Far more often than most Americans like to admit or contemplate, assassination has either threatened or consumed the lives of national leaders. Miami's Bayfront Park provided the setting for one assassin's scenario on February 15, 1933. Guiseppe Zangara chose Franklin D. Roosevelt's brief appearance in the Park that evening as the occasion for an attempt on the president-elect's life. The ensuing eyewitness account of the incident was written by one of Miami's most prominent men, a former mayor and a city resident since the 1890's.

Source: John Sewell, <u>John Sewell's Memoirs and History of Miami, Florida</u> (Miami?: Franklin Press, 1933), 205-210.

When the paper announced that the President-elect would arrive in Miami on the night of February 15th, about 9 o'clock, the city began to arrange to get him to come to Bay Front Park to make a short speech and let the people see him. The President-elect agreed to do as the people wished and everything was arranged.

The Mayor of Miami, Hon. Redmond B. Gautier, was to ride with Governor Roosevelt and introduce him from the car, Mr. George Hussy to introduce the mayor when the party arrived in front of the band shell facing the amphitheater, the party driving around in front of the band shell where all could see and hear over the loud speakers. . . .

A little after eight o'clock the Senator /Senator John W. Watson, sixth mayor of Miami/ came to me where I was standing in the crowd and said they had sent for us. I went with him and his wife to the band shell and located our seats. . . .

/After being seated in the band shell,/ I made a survey of the great crowd, jammed to the limit, every seat taken as well as every inch of standing room. There were acres of human beings, more women than men, all dressed in their best, to see the President-to-be of the United States after March 4th. It was a splendid looking crowd. The weather was warm like a summer evening, and the colored lights and the stately royal palms circling the amphitheater, besides all the thousands of those beautiful women with their beautiful costumes made one of the most beautiful sights that I have ever witnessed. . . .

About 9:25 we could hear the throbs of the motorcycles ridden by the police escort. The next minute the car with police and secret service men came into sight and then the car containing the mayor and the President-elect, Franklin D. Roosevelt. Everyone seemed happy and all lights were turned on to their brightest. Mr. Hussey introduced the mayor, Redmond B. Gautier, he introducing Mr. Roosevelt. Mr. Roosevelt made a short speech, speaking in front of a microphone held by Fred Mizer of Radio Station WQAM. When Mr. Roosevelt finished the whole twenty thousand people were cheering him. He spoke in a most happy vein, promising to come to Miami again. . . . Mr. Roosevelt sat on the folded back top of an open car while speaking, then a huge telegram was brought to him with many thousands of names to it. He slid down into his seat to see the telegram, speaking a few words to Mayor /Anton/ Cermak of Chicago, calling him Tony, asking him to come over to the car. About that time I heard a shot at our right and looked around in that direction and about forty feet from my seat saw a pistol outlined in the air and some bystanders shoving the man's arm up, but the assassin was bending his hand downward, still shooting until the pistol was emptied. About that time three policemen jumped over the first few rows of seats right on top of the man, followed by a bunch of ex-service men with their steel helmets on, and the sheriff Dan Hardie, who was sitting on the band stand with us, was down like a cat. All pounced on top of the assassin and crumpled him up. In the meantime the chauffeur of Mr. Roosevelt's car moved forward out of range, Mr. Roosevelt smiling and waving his hand to let the audience know he was not hurt.

Then I saw blood streaming from a large man with white hair, and also saw two ladies put into the car of secret service men that had come up in the rear of Mr. Roosevelt's car. I saw no blood on the ladies who were put into the car and thought they had fainted. However, when the smoke had cleared away the assassin's bullets had hit five people, Mrs. Joe Gill of Miami, Mayor Cermak of Chicago /who died of his wounds/, the most seriously. Then the great, beautiful, happy audience looked as if a wet blanket had been thrown over it, and the attack of the assassin turned one of the happiest audiences ever assembled in Miami into one of the most sorrowful and indignant, many howling "Kill him, kill him!" Even Mrs. Sewell herself wished for a pistol to shoot the assassin, and that sentiment seemed to be shared by thousands.

A NEW SOLUTION TO MOUNTING METROPOLITAN PROBLEMS
1954

In 1954, the Metropolitan Miami Municipal (3M) Board was assigned the task of studying county and municipal governments in Dade County and drafting a plan for their consolidation or federation. The 3M Board contracted with the University of Miami's Committee on Municipal Research for a fact-finding survey, and the latter group sought out the professional research expertise of Chicago's Public Administration Service. That group published its findigs on December 31, 1954 in The Government of Metropolitan Miami. The report included background on municipal and county government, an analysis of existing problems, and recommendations for federating municipal and county governments in Dade County. From these recommendations "Metro" would emerge by 1957. The brief excerpts from the Public Administration Service's report printed below suggest some of the problems faced by the metropolitan area in 1954 as well as the general outlines of the solution recommended by the research agency.

Source: Public Administration Service, The Government of Metropolitan Miami (Chicago: Public Administration Service, 1954), 35-37, 39-40, 65-67, 85-86. Reprinted by permission of the Public Administration Service.

Public Services in Metropolitan Miami

In the provision of public services, virtually all Miami area communities have lagged far behind the rapid physical growth. Existing sewer systems are inadequate even in the older sections, and little provision is being made for present new development, to say nothing of future expansion. Sewage treatment plants are being built by Miami and Coral Gables, but these cannot be expected to provide the facilities needed by the total metropolitan community, including the unincorporated urban areas of Dade County which are still largely dependent upon septic tanks. Water services are a hodge-podge of public, private, and individual systems constructed to meet immediate problems but with little regard for long-range metropolitan **water requirements either as to sources or distri**bution systems. The very important problem of drainage is dealt with on what amounts to an emergency basis. Virtually every new project involves extensive reconstruction of other facilities and properties disturbed by drainage improvement efforts.

The transportation situation is already acute, with particularly heavy congestion on down-town Miami and Miami Beach streets. The increasing difficulty of moving in and out of the central cities by automobile, plus the absence of adequate public transportation facilities, is clearly promoting more intensive and specialized development of commercial and professional services in the other cities of the metropolitan region. To cope with the traffic problem, however, Miami finds it necessary to set back buildings and widen streets, to construct off-street parking facilities, and to consider the construction of a major network of freeways and arterial boulevards. Such projects are extremely expensive even when heavy land acquisition and clearance costs are not involved. But in the Miami central city region right-of-way costs will indeed be heavy. The problem was not faced clearly enough when the need for wide streets, off-street parking, and even expressways was first foreseen. Now there is real danger that remedial action to solve existing problems will absorb so much attention and revenue that little will be left over to deal with other pressing public problems, much less to anticipate the future needs of a much larger population.

Another basic public service problem is that of providing adequate educational facilities in a community expanding at such a rapid rate as that of Dade County. The public school system, now consolidated into a single county-wide organization, is in far better position by reason of its area-wide coverage to meet its tremendous burden of new construction and employment of additional personnel than if it were composed of a variety of separate and independent districts. The problem is essentially one of developing sufficiently farsighted programs and securing farsighted programs and securing enough funds to keep up with the everexpanding need.

The provision of other public services throughout the Miami metropolitan region involves numerous problems that require attention. Miami itself, and a number of the other incorporated communities have excellent fire protection systems. Equally urbanized areas in some incorporated towns and particularly in unincorporated sections of the county lack adequate fire protection or are dependent upon Miami for it in cases of emergency. Increasingly, as the population of Dade County is augmented by new residents, the older communities, and particularly the central city, are called upon to provide services in areas outside of their respective jurisdictions and without, in return, being able to derive tax support from the areas served. Or, in another way of viewing the same problem, residents of the incorporated communities pay the great bulk of county taxes in order for the county to provide essentially municipal services in unincorporated urban districts. To the extent that basic area-wide services are provided by the municipalities or in unincorporated areas on a service charge basis, citizens throughout the metropolitan region will receive a more equitable distribution of the services they pay for. . . .

The Political Position of the Central City

Within Dade County, as already indicated, are twenty-six municipalities, of which twenty-four are immediately within the Miami urban area. The political units, some small and some of considerable size and population, are so situated as virtually to surround the older central city of Miami. Also, as previously mentioned, population in the neighboring cities and in the unincorporated county area is growing at a more rapid rate than in Miami proper. Miami continues to gain more new residents each year than any other single city in the area, but less than the other incorporated cities taken together and less than the unincorporated portion of the county. Consequently, the City of Miami is gradually losing its dominant position in terms of population. Over a period of time, this loss of position cannot fail to have political consequences. If a clear-cut issue should arise that would pit Miami against the remaining municipalities and the unincorporated areas of the county, Miami would right now lose out at the polls. In 1950 Miami contained just slightly more than fifty per cent of the county's population; today it is estimated to contain less than forty-three per cent. It is even conecivalble that some other of the local communities, by continued population increase accompanied by a series of annexations could come to surpass Miami in residents.

The importance of Miami's position in the midst of a group of incorporated municipalities making up the Greater Miami metropolitan area cannot be overlooked in any proposal for solving existing and future metropolitan problems. Since it is the central city of the region, Mimai's development, prosperity, and program of municipal services are of vital concern to all residents of Dade County. They have a major impact on the basic industry of tourism that benefits the entire southeast Florida region. As is the case with central cities in other metropolitan areas, however, Miami already finds itself faced with the need for undertaking costly and far-reach-

ing improvement projects which will benefit the entire
county but with virtually no assistance from the other
cities and only limited assistance from the county. A
recently proposed highway construction program for reliev-
ing down-town congestion is a case in point.

Problems of the nature just mentioned are not faced
exclusively by Miami in spite of its being the central
city. To a lesser but nevertheless important degree they
must be faced by Coral Gables, Miami Beach, North Miami,
and such other municipalities as now or in the near
future will be called upon to provide a full range of
municipal services. Clearly there is need for a balanced
and over-all view of metropolitan problems and the need
for metropolitan-wide services. Unless steps are taken
to provide such a view and such services, there will be
no alternative to increasing governmental competition,
costly duplication of services and facilities, and an
accelerated impact upon each of the affected communities
of all the difficulties inherent in rapid metropolitan
growth. . . .

The Problem of Government in Summary

There are serious overtones of administraive inept-
ness in the functioning of government in Metropolitan
Miami today, but basically the problem of government stems
from the lack of regional authority and competence to deal
with metropolitan issues. Of the 27 governments in the
area only the county government has a semblance of power
to deal with area-wide problems. But even this limited
power is largely negated by constitutional and statutory
proscriptions. Furthermore, the county's present structure, lacking as it does the basic requisites for the
orderly formulation of policies, good management and sys-
tematic administration, is so cumbersome as to preclude
its effectiveness as an instrument of metropolitan government.

The several municipal governments were intended to
provide only for purely local needs. Although some of
them function adequately in this purpose, none has the
breadth of authority nor the administrative machinery
necessary to cope with regional problems. Even in purely
local objectives their operations are frequently impeded
by the lack of regional coordination, the absence of uniform standards, the unavailability of area-wide public
facilities and utility systems, and by the inadequacy of
public funds.

The citizen of Metropolitan Miami today is faced with
a real dilemma. He has high hopes for the future of the
metropolitan community. He sees the need for, and he
wants better streets and highways, an integrated public
transportation system, improved building and zoning
standards, comprehensive coverage of the area in terms

of water, sewage, and related utility services, better health, welfare, education, recreation, and library programs, and improved law enforcement and fire protection services. He feels, also, frequently with justification, that he pays rather dearly toward the support of local government. Yet in the fulfillment of his aspirations for the community he faces a void. He finds governments in profusion; but upon none can he bring to bear the force of his interests, desires, and determination. It is only natural that this circumstance should be disturbing; but the citizen is even more disturbed in the realization that with the continued rapid growth of the community a prolongation of existing inadequacies can only accentuate the problem of government.

Organizational Alternatives

THERE IS BUT ONE REAL PROBLEM of governmental organization in metropolitan areas. It is the problem of securing a jurisdictional entity with area-wide authority for performing those functions best conducted on a grand scale throughout the area and supported by all the citizens of the area. The reciprocal and complicating feature of the problem is the need to provide within the broad governmental framework adequate latitude for local community structures to continue functioning in the interest of the local citizen and in accordance with his willingness to support services and activities of local benefit distinct from or above the level of service of those normally available from the metropolitan jurisdiction.

Few people who see our cities growing and our population increasing--particularly in those areas which are witnessing very rapid expansion--will deny the ultimate necessity of having some form of local government capable of meeting the needs of an entire metropolitan community. Paradoxically, however, awareness of need has seldom led to a political willingness to act in this sphere of local governmental organization. Questions of method, form, assignment of functions, financing, local tradition, and just plain selfishness all have proved stumbling blocks in the path of effective action. Often legal problems created by state constitutions and state legislation have proved difficult to overcome. . . .

Any plan, if there is any hope for its adoption, must have some tangible benefit to offer a very considerable number of the people. It must be generally acceptable throughout the metropolitan area and in adjacent rural areas. If constitutional change is involved, the plan must make sense to many who may never be directly affected by it; centainly it should have some appeal for those troubled with similar problems in other metropolitan areas of the state. . . .

Combining the Meritorious Features of Various Solutions

There is a recognized and generally accepted need for some form of metropolitan government in the greater Miami area. This need is not now satisfied and will not be satisfied by informal collaboration among the twenty-seven jurisdictions of local government in Dade County. A basic change and improvement in the pattern of local government is essential. All the various possibilities and alternative solutions discussed in the preceding sections of this chapter have their distinct advantages and disadvantages, and fortunately it is not necessary to simply choose one or another. Rather, it is both possible and desirable to select from among the various possibilities in accordance with sound and tested principles of good government, and create for Miami a plan of improvement that will meet virtually all the conditions set forth at the outset of this discussion. In summary, the following steps are recommended.

1. Creation of an area-wide government with jurisdiction throughout the territory of Dade County. Such government should be vested with authority and responsibility for performance of those functions best performed on a regional basis, whether such functions are now performed by municipal units, the various county officials or agencies or not at all.

2. Existing municipal governments should be retained with responsibility for conduct of those functions essentially local in character or which may represent a higher level of service than generally to be provided on an area-wide basis by the metropolitan government.

3. Encouragement should be provided for urban areas in territory not now incorporated to seek annexation to such existing municipal units as local geography dictates and as may be in position to provide local governmental services, or to seek incorporation for provision of their own services.

4. The metropolitan government should provide purely local services throughout its jurisdiction outside of incorporated municipalities on the basis of service charges or special service districts formed for the purpose of paying for such services.

5. The metropolitan government should be construed with an elective legislative body chosen at large from specific representative districts of comparable population, plus representatives selected by the voters of local municipal units possessing at least eight per cent of the population of the metropolitan area. Thus both the general public and the cities of suitable status would be represented in the metropolitan government.

6. The functions, duties, and rights of the existing county government as a fundamental political subdivision

of the State of Florida should be transferred to and vested in the Government of Metropolitan Miami.

7. The basic pattern of the metropolitan government, together with its authority, responsibilities, and duties should be set forth in a charter drawn up and adopted by the residents who are voters in the territory encompassed within the boundaries of the present Dade County.

8. The Constitution of the State of Florida should be amended to provide for the foregoing reorganization of local self-government in Dade County. . . .

METROPOLITAN MIAMI-DADE COUNTY's
HOME RULE CHARTER
1957

On May 21, 1957 Dade County voters approved the Home Rule Charter which federated the county and municipal governments in a structure known as Metro. In one sense, it was the culmination of efforts to establish some sort of metropolitan government in Dade County that dated back to the immediate post-World War II period. In another sense, however, the struggle was far from over. Many embittered controversies, often involving court battles, would disrupt the area's political calm before the relationship between Metro and the municipalities would be defined with any workable precision. Below are printed some significant sections of the Home Rule Charter.

Source: Metropolitan Dade County, Home Rule Charter, 1957.

HOME RULE CHARTER

Preamble

We, the people of this County, in order to secure for ourselves the benefits and responsibilities of home rule, to create a metropolitan government to serve our present and future needs, and to endow our municipalities with the rights of self determination in their local affairs, do under God adopt this home rule Charter,

Article-1
Board of County Commissioners

Section 1.01. Powers
 A. The Board of County Commissioners shall be the legislative and the governing body of the county and shall have the power to carry on a central metropolitan government. This power shall include but shall not be restricted to the power to:
  1. Provide and regulate arterial, toll, and other roads, bridges, tunnels, and related facilities; eliminate grade crossings; provide and regulate parking facilities; and develop and enforce master plans for the control of traffic and parking.

2. Provide and operate air, water, rail, and bus terminals, port facilities, and public transportation systems. . . . .
4. Provide central records, training, and communications for fire and police protection; provide traffic control and central crime investigation; provide fire stations, jails, and related facilities; and subject to Section 1.01A (18) provide a uniform system for fire and police protection.
5. Prepare and enforce comprehensive plans for the development of the county.
6. Provide hospitals and uniform health and welfare programs.
7. Provide parks, preserves, playgrounds, recreation areas, libraries, museums, and other recreational and cultural facilities and programs.
8. Establish and administer housing, slum clearance, urban renewal, conservation, flood and beach erosion control, air pollution control, and drainage programs and cooperate with governmental agencies and private enterprises in the development and operation of these programs.
9. Provide and regulate or permit municipalities to provide and regulate waste and sewage collection and disposal and water supply and conservation programs.
10. Levy and collect taxes and special assessments, borrow money and expend money and issue bonds, revenue certificates, and other obligations of indebtedness in such manner, and subject to such limitations, as may be provided by law.
11. By ordinance, establish, merge, and abolish special purpose districts within which may be provided police and fire protection, beach erosion control, recreation facilities, water, streets, sidewalks, street lighting, waste and sewage collection and disposal, drainage, and other **essential facilities and services.** All county funds for such districts shall be provided by service charges, special assessments, or general tax levies within such districts only. The Board of County Commissioners shall be the governing body of all such districts and when acting as such governing body shall have the same jurisdiction and powers as when acting as the Board.
12. Establish, coordinate, and enforce zoning and such business regulations as are necessary for the protection of the public.
13. Adopt and enforce uniform building and related technical codes and regulations for both the incorporated and unincorporated areas of the coun-

ty; provide for examinations for contractors and all parties engaged in the building trades and for the issuance of certificates of competency and their revocation after hearing. Such certificates shall be recognized and required for the issuance of a license in all municipalities in the county. No municipality shall be entitled to require examinations or any additional certificate of competency or impose any other conditions for the issuance of a municipal license except the payment of the customary fee.

. . .

14. Regulate, control, take over, and grant franchises to, or itself operate gas, light, power, telephone, and other utilities, sanitary and sewage collection and disposal systems, water supply, treatment, and service systems, and public transportation systems, provided, however, that:
    (a) Franchises under this subsection may only be granted by a two-thirds vote of the members of the Board present and approved by a majority vote of those qualified electors voting at either a special or general election.
    (b) The county shall not operate a light, power, or telephone utility to serve any territory in the county which is being supplied with similar service except by a majority vote of those qualified electors voting in an election held not less than six months after the Board has passed an ordinance to that effect by a two-thirds vote of the members of the Board present. Such ordinance shall contain information on cost, method of financing, agency to regulate rates, agency to operate, location, and other information necessary to inform the general public of the feasibility and practicality of the proposed operation.
15. Use public funds for the purposes of promoting the development of the county, including advertising the area's advantages.
16. Establish and enforce regulations for the sale of alcoholic beverages.
17. Enter into contracts with other governmental units within or outside the boundaries of the county for joint performance or performance by one unit in behalf of the other of any authorized function.
18. Set reasonable minimum standards for all governmental units in the county for the performance of any service or function. The standards shall not be discriminatory as between similar areas. If a governmental unit fails to comply with such

standards, and does not correct such failure after reasonable notice by the Board, then the Board may take over and perform, regulate, or grant franchises to operate any such service. The Board may also take over and operate or grant franchises to operate any municipal service if:

(a) In an election called by the Board of County Commissioners within the municipality a majority of those voting vote in favor of turning the service over to the county; or

(b) The governing body of the municipality requests the county to take over the service by a two-thirds vote of its members, or by referendum.

19. (a) By ordinance, abolish or consolidate the office of constables, or any county office created by the Legislature, or provide for the consolidation and transfer of any of the functions of such officers, provided, however, that there shall be no power to abolish the Superintendent of Public Instruction, Sheriff, or to abolish or impair the jurisdiction of the Circuit Court or to abolish any other Court, provided by the Constitution or by general law, or the judges or clerks thereof.

20. Make investigations of county affairs, inquire into the conduct, accounts, records, and transactions of any department or office of the county, and for these purposes require reports from all county officers and employees, subpoena witnesses, administer oaths, and require the production of records.

21. Exercise all powers and privileges granted to municipalities, counties, and county officers by the Constitution and laws of the state, and all powers not prohibited by the Constitution or by this Charter.

22. Adopt such ordinances and resolutions as may be required in the exercise of its powers, and prescribe fines and penalties for the violation of ordinances.

23. Perform any other acts consistent with law which are required by this Charter or which are in the common interest of the people of the county.

24. Supersede, nullify, or amend any special law applying to this county, or any general law applying only to this county, or any general law where specifically authorized by the Constitution.

B. No enumeration of powers in this Charter shall be deemed exclusive or restrictive and the foregoing powers shall be deemed to include all implied powers necessary and proper to carrying out such powers. All of these powers may be exercised in the incorporated and unincorporated areas, subject to the procedures herein provided in certain cases relating to municipalities.

* * *

Section 1.03. Districts /as amended by voters on 11-5-63/
    A. There shall be eight County Commission districts.

* * *

    B. The Board may by ordinance adopted by two-thirds vote of the members of the Board change the boundaries of the districts from time to time. The boundaries shall be fixed on the basis of the character, population, and geography of the districts.

Section 1.04. Composition of the Board. /as amended by voters on 11-5-63/
The Board shall consist of nine members elected as follows:
1. From each of the eight districts there shall be elected by the qualified electors of the county at large a County Commissioner who shall be a qualified elector residing within the district at least six months and within the county at least three years before qualifying.
2. There shall be elected by the qualified electors of the county at large a Mayor who shall be a qualified elector residing within the county at least three years before qualifying. The Mayor shall also serve as a member of the Board and shall be subject to all restrictions provided in this Charter applying to all other Commissioners.

Beginning with the state primary elections in 1968, the Mayor and each Commissioner shall be elected for a term of four years.

* * *

Article-2
Elections

Section 2.03. Nonpartisan Elections.
    All elections for Mayor and the other members of the Board shall be nonpartisan and no ballot shall show the party designation of any candidate. No candidate shall be required to pay any party assessment or state the party of which he is a member or the manner in which he voted or will vote in any election. . . . .

Article-3
The County Manager

Section 3.01. Appointment and Removal
    The Board of County Commissioners shall appoint a County Manager who shall be the chief executive officer

and head of the administraive branch of the county government. The Board shall fix the Manager's compensation, and he shall serve at the will of the Board.

Section 3.02. Qualifications.
 The Manager shall be chosen by the Board on the basis of his executive and administraive qualification. At the time of his appointment he need not be a resident of the state. No County Commissioner shall be eligible for the position of Manager during or within two years after the expiration of his latest term as Commissioner.

* * *

Section 3.04. Powers and Duties.
 A. The Manager shall be responsible to the Board of County Commissioners for the administration of all units of the county government under his jurisdiction, and for carrying out policies adopted by the Board. The Manager, or such other persons as may be designated by resolution of the Board, shall execute contracts and other instruments, sign bonds and other evidences of indebtedness, and accept process.
 B. Unless otherwise provided for by civil service rules and regulations, the Manager shall have the power to appoint and suspend all administrative department heads of the major departments if the county, to-wit: Tax Collector, Tax Assessor, Department of Public Works, Department of Public Safety, Building and Zoning Department, Planning Department, Finance Department, Park and Recreation Department and Internal Auditing Department, except that before any appointment shall become effective, the said appointment must be approved by the County Commission and if the same is disapproved the said appointment shall be void. In the event such appointment shall be disapproved by the County Commission the appointment shall forthright become null and void and thereupon the County Manager shall make a new appointment or appointments, each of which shall likewise be submitted for approval by the County Commission. However, the right to suspend, remove or discharge any department head with or without cause, is reserved at all times to the County Manager.

Section 3.05. Restriction on Board Members.
 Neither the Board nor any of its members, shall direct or request the appointment of any person to, or his removal from, office by the Manager or any of his subordinates, or take part in the appointment or removal of officers and employees in the administrative services of the county. Except for the purpose of inquiry, as provided in Section 1.01 A (20), the Board and its members shall deal with the administrative service solely through the Manager and neither the Board nor any members thereof shall give orders to any subordinates of the Manager,

either publicly or privately. Any wilful violation of the provisions of this Section by a member of the Board shall be grounds for his removal from office by an action brought in the Circuit Court by the State Attorney of this county.

* * *

Article-5
Municipalities

Section 5.01. Continuance of Municipalities.

The municipalities in the County shall remain in existence so long as their electors desire. No municipality in the county shall be abolished without approval of a majority of its electors voting in an election called for that purpose. The right of self determination in local affairs is reserved and preserved to the municipalities except as otherwise provided in this Charter.

Section 5.02. Municipal Powers.

Each municipality shall have the authority to exercise all powers relating to its local affairs not inconsistent with this Charter. Each municipality may provide for higher standards of zoning, service, and regulation than those provided by the Board of County Commissioners in order that its individual character and standards may be preserved for its citizens.

* * *

Article-7
Initiative, Referendum, and Recall

Section 7.01. Initiative and Referendum.

The electors of the county shall have the power to propose to the Board of County Commissioners passage or repeal of ordinances and to vote on the question if the Board refuses action, according to the following procedure:

1. The person proposing the exercise of this power shall submit the proposal to the Board which shall without delay approve as to form a petition for circulation in one or several copies as the proper may desire.
2. The person or persons circulating the petition shall, within one month of the approval of the form of the petition, obtain the signatures of voters in numbers at least equal to ten percent of the total vote in the county for the office of Governor at the last preceding gubernatorial general election. . . .

* * *

4. The Board shall within 30 days after the date a sufficient petition is presented either:

(a) Adopt the ordinance as submitted in an initiatory petition or repeal the ordinance referred to by a referendary petition, or
(b) Determine to submit the proposal to the electors.
5. The vote of the electors, if required, shall take place within 120 days after the date the petition is presented to the Board, preferably in an election already scheduled for other purposes, otherwise in a special election. The result shall be determined by a majority vote of the electors voting on the proposal.
6. An ordinance proposed by initiatory petition or the repeal of an ordinance by referendary petition shall be effective on the day after the election, except that:
(a) Any reduction or elimination of existing revenue or any expenditures not provided for by the current budget or existing bond issues shall not take effect until the beginning of the next succeeding fiscal year. . . .
* * *
(c) Should two or more ordinances adopted at the same election have conflicting provisions, the one receiving the highest number of votes shall prevail as to those provisions.
7. An ordinance adopted by the electorate through initiatory proceedings shall not be amended or repealed by the Board for a period of one year after the election at which it was adopted, but thereafter it may be amended or repealed like any other ordinance.

METRO AND THE CHALLENGE OF LOCALISM
1958

Metro's implementation immediately aroused controversy over what were county-wide functions and services and, therefore, under Metro's control, and what were local matters and, therefore, under the control of the separate municipalities. It was a thorny problem, the solution of which would only emerge from a series of court decisions and the day-to-day interaction between Metro and local governing bodies. In the meantime, opponents of Metro tried to hedge its powers. The editorial below is from the Miami Herald, a consistent Metro booster. It urged Metro officials to curtail the expansion of municipal government activities in areas where Metro could act more effectively and economically.

Source: Miami Herald, December 31, 1958, 4-A.

BACK ON THE COURSE, METRO!

The 12 men in charge of Metropolitan Government here ought to do a little soul-searching this New Year's Eve. We mean the 11 Metro Commissioners and their chief executive, County Manager O. W. Campbell.

Their job is to get rid of duplication and overlapping in local government, improve efficiency and stop waste. That is what the people have voted for no less than four times.

Yet what has been happening? The Dade County League of Municipalities, made up of city office holders, has been indoctrinating the commissioners and Campbell with the theory that Metro should be just another government on top of all the others here.

So effective has been the constant dingdonging of this line that the 12 top men of Metro seem to be sinking into a featherbed of peaceful coexistence with the league.

As a result, municipalities - particularly the City of Miami - keep branching out, adding more people to the payroll, loading more expenses on their tax payers, under the permissive eye of Metro, which can and should be doing much of this work better and cheaper.

Things have gone so far that Metro officials now are

120   MIAMI

talking about setting up new "cities," numbered instead
of named, in unincorporated territory. The only possible
merit of such a step would be to retrieve the cigaret
tax and any other rebatable monies being sent to Tallahassee. Cigaret taxes collected inside city limits go to
the municipalities, while the rest are kept by the state.

Keeping this money at home is a worthy aim, but
people will take a dim view of doing it by creating another layer of potential bureaucracy.

This is the antithesis of what the voters have demanded four times at the polls. They are waiting for
Metro to streamline the whole structure of government for
efficiency and economy.

Let the Metro commissioners and County Manager Campbell start the New Year right. They can do so by getting
back on the straight course pointed out to them emphatically and repeatedly by the people.

DIVERSIFYING MIAMI'S ECONOMY
1965

During the 1960's one of Metropolitan Miami's most significant economic developments involved an aggressive effort to attract industry to the area. From the 1920's onward, the region's economy reflected almost exclusively the imperatives of tourism. Undoubtedly, the city realized substantial benefits, but the single-minded emphasis on tourism imposed severe seasonal and structural strictures on the area's growth. Recognizing this, Metro spearheaded the drive toward diversification by creating the Dade County Development Department to promote industrialization. The comments below describe some of the promotional efforts along with Miami's assets and liabilities as an industrial center.

Source: New York Times, May 2, 1965, Sect. III, pp. 1, 9.

 Five years ago the North Shore Nameplate Company, which made name plates and did short-run job printing was situated in Bayside, Queens. Its annual volume was under $500,000.
 Today, reborn as Anodyne, Inc., and relocated in a modern, sprawling plant at Sunshine State Industrial Park here, the company is a major world manufacturer of multi-colored anodized aluminum. Sales in its latest fiscal year rose almost 45 per cent to $1.5 million.
 Anodyne's growth and development symbolize what has been happening here in the 27 municipalities known collectively as Metropolitan Miami in the last decade. For this well-known bastion of tourism has become the industrial center of Florida and an important industrial factor on the national scene.
 "And we're looking forward to an even greater in-depth expansion in the future," says William J. Branigan, who last month became director of the Dade County Development Department, an official agency of this area's "metro" government. 1964 was certainly the year that was -- industrially speaking. Half of the 700 new plants and major expansions in all of Florida took place here, bringing the total number of Miami-area manufacturers to 3,200.

These new plants brought 4,500 new jobs for the 1.1 million population and 420,000 in the permanent labor force of Metropolitan Miami, also the top figure for the state. Currently the principal industries are foods, printing, metal products, apparel and furniture.

As a result of this surge, Dade County leads the nation in the rate of increase in manufacturing plants, manufacturing employment, manufacturing payrolls and value added by manufacturers.

The outlook for 1965 is even better, at least from the point of view of the development department. It forecasts that 370 new plants, with an initial employment of 5,500, will begin operations in the county during the year.

What's behind this boom in South Florida industrial development? Ask Elmer E. Nelson, plant manager of the Aerojet-Dade division of the Aerojet-General Corporation why his company set up its new solid-propellant rocket-motor facility on a 75,000-acre site in Homestead.

"We wanted to find a large block of land with access to deep water and as close to Cape Kennedy as price and other things would permit," he says. "We also wanted a place with all the amenities -- a nice place to live, schools, universities, etc."

Climate Cited

Ask Philip Bernstein, vice president of the Victory Electronics and Research Corporation, why his company moved here from Chicago last year.

"Ninety-nine per cent of all business people would like to be down here from a climate standpoint," he answers. "And the development department is doing everything possible to help new people in the area."

For municipal and county officials, the luring of new industries helps to reduce Dade County's overdependence on its largest single employer--tourism. Besides that, every new company provides additional employment opportunities and stimulates existing concerns in the environs.

But getting companies to move from their present locations to Florida is no easy task. Many corporations, especially smaller ones, have the view, as expressed by one New York industrial properties specialist, that "moving more than a couple of hundred miles away usually causes trouble."

Officials here realize, too, that the location of an industrial plant generally requires a lead time of two to five years. On top of that, Florida offers no "artificial concessions" like reduced taxes, free land or free buildings because, in the words of a state official, "industry wants to be a paying member of the community. Really solid industry wants to carry its load."

There is also the severe competition for new industry.

Estimates of the number of agencies--state, local, chamber of commerce, nonprofit and private--seeking plants for their areas range from 9,000 to more than 14,000. There are 350 known industrial-development organizations in Florida alone.

Then there are the acknowledged liabilities of the Miami region as a plant site. Perhaps the greatest is the reputation of the city, Miami Beach and other communities in this general area as one of the nation's leading vacation resorts.

As the development department itself admits, "few non-management stockholders can visualize their company locating a plant here. These stockholders no more think of industry located in Miami than they think of churches located in Las Vegas, although both exist."

In addition, the area has an extreme geographical location at the tip of a peninsula in the southern part of the country, personal property taxes are levied on inventory and machinery, land costs are high and there is one of the highest congestion rates in the United States.

Yet many companies whose managements are sophisticated and knowledgeable in the ways of business and finance have obviously relocated in Metropolitan Miami.

One big reason for this is that officials here are actively selling their product in many ways. For example, in March, officials of the Florida Development Commission went to New York to keep some 200 prearranged appointments with executives who were attending a convention of the Institute of Electrical and Electronic Engineers.

The city of Coral Gables, one of the units within Metropolitan Miami, has its own separate community development department and its director, Jack D. Sutter, makes similar trips to New York. In fact, it was on a trip to an I.E.E.E. convention by Miami officials that Victory Electronics first began exploring the possibility of relocating.

Dade County's development department looks upon the contacts with industrial prospects as more than just a sometime thing. In addition to working closely with the Committee of 21 of the Miami-Dade County Chamber of Commerce's Industrial Development Council, its arsenal includes three full-time out-of-state representatives.

These men, with headquarters in Philadelphia, Chicago and Boston, visit companies in their territories on a day-to-day basis. The reports they file with Miami are similar to those used by many industrial salesmen and enable the headquarters office to keep track of their activities.

Metropolitan Miami also advertises its wares--such as 100 per cent plant financing, a variety of industrial parks and the lack of a state income tax--in such publications as the Wall Street Journal, Fortune, Business Week, and various trade magazines. Its space budget in the current fiscal year is $45,000.

Both the salesmen and the media ads boast of the economic assets in Dade County. These include a skilled labor force, expanding markets, excellent air transport facilities--and, of course, the Miami weather, for which winter vacationists pay large sums of money.

Weather is such an important factor to the development people here that they concentrate their most important sales calls in the fall and winter when Northern businessmen are likely to be most susceptible to the blandishments of Southern living.

Eugene T. Turney, Jr., the ebullient gray-haired president of Anodyne, is a transplanted New Yorker who today boosts the industrial development of south Florida like a native. Seated in his spacious office under a mounted sailfish caught in Florida waters and gazing toward his fenced-in Polynesian garden, he ticks off what he believes to be the industrial advantages here.

"This is a creative climate because anyone who is creative thrives with a climate that goes with his biological personality. It's a 365-days-a-year operation because there is no absenteeism due to bad weather. Wages are stable all year long because there are no production hills and valleys."

Another big industrial advantage he sees is that "all the people we want to do business with come here to vacation. We invite them to visit our plant. We even bring them out here, and we get a lot of business that way."

As might be expected, not every businessman here takes the Chamber of Commerce view about Miami's industrial scene. One executive says, "we're banking a lot on new industry coming down. Right now, we have to go to the East and Midwest for a lot of material. We're hoping that in time it will be made down here or suppliers of ours will move here."

Even the public relations man for a company here will say guardedly that "the community isn't really industry-oriented. They think too much about tourism."

But with the construction of about 700 new plants and 49 miles of expressway in the last 10 years, with the backing of an industry-minded Metropolitan Dade County government, and with the interest of almost 2,000 more labor-oriented, tourist-compatible companies already piqued, the future looks bright for still further industrial gains in this land of sand, surf and palm trees.

CHIEF HEADLEY GETS TOUGH
1968

While the history of Miami's Black population is marked by the same deprivations and frustrations that have produced massive violence in several major American cities, Dade County residents remained generally unaware of the strained situation until the summer of 1967. During the heat of those months, Miamians watched apprehensively as riots threatened to break out several times. That peace prevailed is a credit to both the Black and the white local leaders. Despite numerous promises for remedial action, however, the tension-producing conditions were not alleviated and the long-feared explosion came in August 1968. Between December 1967 and August 1968, the race situation was aggravated by the "get tough" policy of Miami Police Chief Walter Headley. Disturbed by the disproportionate incidence of crime in Black sections of Miami, Headley began equipping his men with dogs and shotguns. The Miami Herald article below followed the implementation of Headley's controversial policy by about a month. It describes the tactics of the police and some of the results of and reactions to Headley's crackdown.

Source: Miami Herald, January 29, 1968.

Patrolman L. D. Putman rides the Central Negro District from 10 a.m. to 6 p.m. A German shepherd named Lad shares his cruiser.

Putman went into the central district almost a month ago. He is part of the extra force dispatched into Miami's Negro areas by Police Chief Walter Headley in a crack down on what the chief called "young hoodlums taking advantage of the civil rights movement."

The streets are safer now.

Police statistics show it. And the change is easy to see. The young men who clustered on the sidewalk of Second Avenue even in the daytime aren't there now. The green-and-white patrol cars with steel mesh between front and back seats are much more in evidence.

The merchants, the women, the winos who used to be attacked are grateful to the police, even the white one like Putman.

But Putman, a man who is concerned about such things, thinks he is also winning the acceptance and grudging respect of the young men.

There's evidence he's wrong.

"The cops are taking advantage of the situation. My friends have been harassed in bars and pool rooms. People are staying in more.

"They will eventually get tired and say to hell with it."

The speaker was a 23-year-old resident of NW First Ave. He was angry and sullen. His mood is widely shared.

It WORRIES many people who work with that intangible called community relations, but it does not appear to worry greatly Headley or his field commanders.

This heat's going to go on as long as we've got the public with us," said Lt. Charles Renegar, commander of the 60-man task force to which Putman is attached.

The strategy being followed by the task force is based on their conclusion that the crimes of violence prevalent in the Negro areas are perpetrated by the gangs of "Negro males aged 15 to 25" who hang on the street corners and in the bars and pool rooms.

The victims, a study of the records showed, were in most cases purse-carrying women, helpless drunks and, less frequently, shopkeepers and deliverymen.

Many of the strong-arm crimes were committed in broad daylight.

So Putman and two other "dogmen" now patrol the central district in the daytime, when one man formerly was there. The dogs are kept in the vehicles, except for brief exercise walks or occasions when a building is checked. They are a deterrent force, there to see and, more important, be seen.

Putman keeps a notebook, jotting down names and descriptions of everybody he talks to. When one youth asked why, he smiled.

"I want to know you the next time I see you."

Canine cars also work the Liberty City area.

* * *

AT NIGHT, the rest of the task force goes to work. Traveling in teams, shotguns in their cars but not used so far, the officers roam the "high crime" zones.

They break up street-corner groups and enter poolhalls and bars to demand identification from the patrons. There are arrests for vagrancy and more serious offenses.

Intent of all this is to disturb the potential troublemakers, make them change their ways of operation and keep them under surveillance.

The police, the people they are out to protect, even

the people who see themselves as persecuted all agree that the gangs have been broken up, at least for the moment. The incidence of violent crime is down dramatically from December.

"It takes fear out of me -- just the fact that he comes around," Mrs. Carrie Morley said of the officer newly assigned to the area around her tiny grocery store on NW 17th St.

She has been robbed once, at gunpoint.

Henry Ross, a beer truck driver, agreed that Headley has finally taken a step long overdue.

"There's no other way it can be done. Otherwise, it's not safe to walk the streets. You can't live in peace."

Ross has been held up three times in six months.

* * *

"IF IT GETS any worse, I'm gonna have to quit my job. I got a family to support. I can't lose my life."

David McMillan, 50, manages Clyde's Recreation on Second Ave.

"I don't see any harm in the policy myself. We all knew something had to be done. The police don't bother me personally.

"I get along with both law and hoodlums. For Second Ave. it's done a whole lot."

Fear lives with many residents of the ghettoes.

"From the time the sun goes down I'm scared to go out unless I got something in my hand," said 62-year-old John Rawls.

"You can't walk Third Ave, unless you got a gun."

More police mean fewer "jitterbugs" on the corner to Rawls.

"Since the police been around here, you don't see too many of 'em."

There is another side to the **story**, though. The view is different from the sidewalk.

A HERALD REPORTER was talking with several men on a corner in the Central Negro District early one night when a car with two policemen drove up.

"Give me this sidewalk," said one officer. Several of the men accepted without argument his order to disperse.

Two who didn't were ordered to the car to produce identification. The reporter, himself a Negro, and another man continued talking. One of the policemen motioned them to the car.

"I was just talking to this reporter here," the man said.

The policeman looked surprised, said "Oh, I didn't recognize you" to the reporter, and drove away.

A teenager said several boys were standing on a corner when two officers came up and ordered tham to put their hands on the wall to be searched.

"One boy jumped like he was being tickled by the officer," the youth said, "and this cop with a shotgun cocked it and said, 'Boy, you better be still 'cause this gun goes off very easily.'"

James Jackson, 17, said, "I got stopped when I was going home from Royal Castle. Asked me where I was going. Some of them when they stop you will get nasty and start cursing.

* * *

"COLORED policemen are doing that just because whitey is pushing them.

"They took me to jail one time for loitering. I just walked into the poolroom and this cop took me by the arm and told be to stand by the wall.

"I stayed in jail four days for it. All he asked for was an ID and I had that. I asked why he was taking me to jail and he said they had to do something."

"Then he drove me over by Sixth Ave. and told me to get out of the car and he said 'When I count to three I want you to get out and run.'

"So I got out and started walking and he called me back and said 'Did you hear what I said?' so I started running."

Lt. Renegar said his men never take shotguns into the places they check out.

He also said, "I have yet to receive any complaint about any of my men conducting these searches."

* * *

MORE important than whether Hepburn's and Jackson's stories are wholly or even partially true is that they are being told and believed among those who consider police their natural enemies.

Headley and his men are taking no great pains to ease that impression.

Edward Hepburn, 18, told a similar story:

"I was shooting pool and this sergeant came to the door with another officer who came in the back door with a shotgun. Everybody stopped playing but me and the sergeant said "When you see me coming I want you to stop.'

"So I asked him why and he said 'cause you're my enemy.' He put me in his car and told me 'when I talk to you I want you to talk to me nice,' so I started saying yessir.

Renegar considers the publicity given the chief's "shotguns and dogs" announcement "one of the best things that's happened to the police force."

Some important elements of the public are disturbed by the racial overtones they heard in Headley's words, however.

Several Negro members of the Community Relations Board said they have received complaints of police "harrassment" and discourtesy.

Both Negro and white members, while declining to be

quoted by name, said privately and emphatically they were particularly upset that Headley chose not to take the opportunity offered him by CRB chairman Harry Cain to remove the racial sting from his Dec. 26 announcement.

They cited by comparison figures showing that crime increased only one-fourth as much last year in that part of the Liberty City-Brownsville area patrolled by the Sheriff's Department as in the rest of Dade County.

Sheriff E. Wilson Purdy has devoted intensive community relations efforts to that area.

Community relations, Negro leaders say, has never been a strong point of the Miami Police Department. Headley appears to have put his faith in tough action rather than soft words.

* * *

THERE IS a question, at least in the minds of many in the ghettoes, how long the crackdown will last.

Renegar insists it can and will go on indefinitely. Most of the men being used were already assigned to his task force, which he calls the department's "mobile striking force."

The canine men are now working six-day weeks but Renegar says more dogs are being trained to ease that shortage.

Still, some of the older people fear, and some of the younger ones are counting on, an easing of the pressure sooner or later.

One policeman speculated that the intensive effort will be called off in a month or so and then reapplied if gang activity increases again.

The most important question -- since most of the white community seems to be behind Headley -- may be whether the angry young Negroes will come to accept the behavior patterns the police are trying to force on them.

LIBERTY CITY ROCKED BY RIOTS
1968

The fuse in Miami's black community which had run dangerously short during 1967, ran out on August 7, 1968 as disorder spread through the Liberty City section. Two days of disturbances left three dead (a fourth death came on August 13 in the Coconut Grove district) and many more injured. Although the Republican National Convention was meeting at the same time in Miami Beach, a report sponsored by the National Commission on the Causes and Prevention of Violence concluded that the riot's roots were neither political nore ideological in nature. The government study team's conclusions on the causes of the riots are printed below, along with sections of their <u>Miami Report</u> which describe the Liberty City locale and analyze some of the factors involved in the violence.

Source: National Commission on the Causes and Prevention of Violence, <u>Miami Report</u> (Washington, D.C.: U.S. Government Printing Office, 1969), viii, 1-2, 25-27.

The Riot Area

    The Miami distrubances took place almost entirely within the Liberty City section of the City of Miami. Miami is located in Dade County, Florida, and Liberty City on its west side lies directly along the boundary between the City of Miami and the unincorporated area of Dade County. Police protection within the city is provided by the City of Miami police; within the unincorporated area by the Dade County Department of Public Safety, also known as the Dade County Sheriff's Department.
    Liberty City is a black area with a population of approximately 45,000 located in the northwest section of the City of Miami. It was planned after World War II as a model locost housing area to supplement and eventually replace the old Central Negro District of dilapidated wooden houses. In its early stages it consisted of low, widely-spaced buildings with ample green space between them, but in succeeding years the area has come more and more to be filled with what are locally called "concrete

monsters," i.e., multi-storied concrete block apartment houses with open balconies entirely surrounded by asphalt paved areas. A lack of effective planning and zoning controls, lax enforcement of health, sanitation, and maintenance standards and the substantial profits to be derived from the construction and rental of high-density low-maintenance apartment units have destroyed the original concept of a more civilized and liveable low-cost housing area. Ironically, one of the reasons for the high population concentration in the Liberty City area has been the displacement of blacks from other areas by various urban renewal and improvement projects, without adequate housing provisions having been made for them elsewhere.

As the Libert City area has become more and more built up over recent years, the concentration of people, noise, and, in August, heat, has made living conditions there less and less tolerable.

* * *

The fact that the Republican National Convention was taking place during the week of August 5th, at Miami Beach, some seven miles away from Liberty City, played only an incidental part in the course of the disturbances. The disturbances involved no articulated political or ideological issues such as the Presidential campaign, Viet Nam or the draft. The disturbances were preceded by two attempts to hold mass rallies, but neither of these was particularly successful, and the leaders of the rallies did not play a significant part in the disturbances. Although the slogan "Black Power" and the characteristic raised-fist gesture were used on numerous occasions during the disturbances, they were used as expressions of solidarity and emotional fervor by the participants and not as a part of a planned confrontation or demonstration to obtain specific governmental or economic reforms.

* * *

The disturbances originated spontaneously and almost entirely out of the accumulated deprivations, discriminations, and frustrations of the black community in Liberty City, which are similar to those of urban black communities throughout the United States, exacerbated by the following special local circumstances:

(a) Loss of local jobs by blacks over the prior several years to Cuban refugees.

(b) Failure of the Dade County business community during the summers of 1967 and 1968 to provide a sufficient number of jobs for black youths despite widely publicized promises to do so.

(c) Tensions of many years standing between the Miami black community and the Miami police, which had sharply increased in recent months.

* * *

Disorder and Riot

Chapter 4 of our Report /discussing events on August 7/ is entitled, perhaps with undue drama, "The Riot Starts." This is a short-handed way of describing our general observation that what took place before then was a rather harmless and not uncommon type of expression of grievances combined with general exuberance and letting off of steam. It could have been quickly checked or controlled at almost any point of time by a firm, properly organized display of adequate force. Although some of the characteristic black power manifestations were in evidence, there was none of the virulence, irrationality, and almost obsessive law-breaking characteristic of riots as we understand them. In many ways, these earlier actions seem to have been more characteristic of an overexuberant crowd at a hotly-contested sporting event which police can keep within reasonable bounds, or perhaps more aptly, a tense labor relations confrontation. This is not meant to denigrate the very real convictions of social, economic and political injustice which lie at the basis of protest meetings. . . and the subsequent disorders, The point is rather that despite very real convictions of injustice, their expression is often accomplished with physical restraint even when accompanied by verba, excesses, which indeed themselves are often used with a certain tongue-in-cheek attitude.

* * *

Press, Radio and TV

We have no doubt that the prompt dissemination of news concerning the development of a riot may itself have an effect on the riot. In Miami, the broadcasting of the news, sometimes live from the spot, served to attract outsiders of the area, some bent on rioting and looting and others merely attracted by the excitement. This no doubt enlarges the riot and thereby makes the control job harder. The conflict thus created between the maintaining of civil order and the free gathering and transmission of news is simple, classic, and difficult to resolve. We do not purport to add anything to the conventional wisdom in this area.

A more recent and perhaps more difficult problem is whether the very presence of news media, particularly TV cameras, at the scene of violence increases the amount of intensity of the violence. On this point, we find the sharpest disagreement. Most police testimony is that it does and that it "impedes law enforcemen." Black leaders claim that it does not. Our investigation found very little evidence on the point. . . .

Our conclusions on the communications media are disappointingly meager. The Miami rioters were not consciously seeking publicity as were those in Chicago, and they apparently had no plans to embarras the police by provoking them to take unusually strong action in view of TV cameras. If we assume the basic decision that a riot can freely be reported even if this brings more rioters to the area, we do not see from our limited experiences that the presence of the communications media significantly encourages or magnifies the violence unless the rioters are rioting at least in part for the very purpose of massive TV coverage.

Terror vs. Force

It is not unfair to characterize the Headley policy as one of keeping an underprivileged and restless minority orderly and cowed by a constant visual display of force in its more ominous and symbolic forms, e.g., shotguns and police dogs, coupled with frequent harshly-executed acts of stopping and frisking or stopping for questioning, and whether consciously planned or not, occasional acts of brutality. Quite apart from more basic legal and ethical problems, the greatest failings of this policy are that it creates grievances which can accumulate until they actually cause a riot and that the training and equipping of police for the application of such a policy does not prepare them to cope with a major riot without widespread indiscriminate and useless bloodshed and simultaneously sowing the seeds for future disturbances. And once a riot starts, police dogs sitting in their mobile cages or shotguns sticking out of the windows of police cars--the most usual modes of display--will have little or no effect on the rioters.

Many of the City of Miami police officers who were at the disturbance seem to be aware of this, at least in part. Almost uniformly they ask for more and better riot control equipment. Some of the items they request seem somewhat more suited for outright war than for riot control, but we think they are right in principle that riot prevention and control needs special equipment in adequate quantities and that this means something more than shotguns and police dogs. We think, in short, that the use of instruments of terror to hold potential disturbances in check eventually fails to hold them in check and then is of little or no use in quelling a disturbance once it starts.

It is interesting also to note that many of the Miami Police officers in their reports complain of the confusion and lack of organization and planning in the initial stages of the Miami Police efforts to prevent and then control the riot. The picture of totally uncoordinated Miami squad cars racing from spot to spot with sirens screaming which is implied in some reports is undoubtedly exaggerated, but it is clear that many of the Miami Police were very dissatisfied with the lack of planning and coordination by the Police Department. In our judgment, this is not unrelated to the basic get-tough, show-of-force policy. Such a policy by its very nature discourages contacts with the potential rioters, knowledge of their psychology, and sensitivity to how and where disturbances may break out. Since it relies basically on frightening or cowing individuals or small groups by symbolic or token violence, it takes little account of disorderly and riotous masses of people who may react in exactly the opposite way to such attitudes and practices.

We do not purport to judge whether the City of Miami police could have eventually brought the Libert City disturbance under control or how long it would have taken. We do conclude, however, that there was a basic and important difference between their anti-riot actions and the Sheriff's /Sheriff E. Purdy Wilson, Dade County Public Safety Department/ use of a force of well-armed and trained police and soldiers equipped with full anti-riot equipment proceeding, according to a clearly defined and understood plan, to completely clear the area of disturbance with the use only of that force necessary to accomplish the objective.

We do not conclude that the disturbances would not have taken place had the Sheriff been in charge of Liberty City at all times. We do conclude that long-term community relations programs and planning against the contingency of disturbances or riots on the part of the Sheriff were substantially better than those of the Miami Police and that had the Sheriff been in charge of Liberty City at all times the disturbances might not have gotten out of hand. We do conclude that as events transpired, the City of Miami could well have asked at an earlier time for outside assistance to secure a massive presence of armed force and that the Sheriff's general strategy of stopping a riot once it has started was demonstrably superior to that used by the City.

Black Police

There appears to be no effective and continuous policy on the part of the City of Miami to encourage recruitment of qualified blacks as members of its police force, although a substantial portion of the population of the city is black. It also appears that the comparatively few black members of the force, for reasons unexplained, do not progress upwards through the ranks to positions of administrative and command responsibility. The leaders of the black community feel strongly that well-trained and motivated black police would be a powerful riot preventative and positive community relations factor, particularly if some black police occupied positions of responsibility on the force. There seems to be no substantial feeling that blacks should be promoted just because they are black, but there is a real conviction that a qualified black policeman does not get the same "break" as an equivalently qualified white. In view of this attitude of the black leaders and the black community it would appear that this is a matter deserving of serious consideration and affirmative action.

CUBANS PROSPER IN MIAMI
1969

Miami's geographic proximity to Cuba made it a logical residential center for exiles after Fidel Castro's takeover. As the refugee tide swelled, especially with the post-1965 "freedom flights," many Miamians grew apprehensive about social and economic problems that they anticipated. Economically, there was particular concern over potential Cuban-black competition for the limited number of jobs generated by the tourist trade. These fears proved largely unfounded since many Cubans arrived with marketable technological and/or intellectual skills. Their economic impact proved revitalizing rather than burdensome. The mini-biographies in the following article illustrate how man Cuban immigrants, including Cuban blacks, have prospered as individuals and have contributed as a group to Miami's growth.

Source: New York Times, January 26, 1969, p. 15.

Jose O. Padron, a 36 year old Cuban refugee, arrived here penniless in 1962. A third generation tobacco grower from Pinar del Rio, one of the most celebrated tobacco areas in the world, he could find only odd manual jobs to support his wife and three children.

About three years later, with $600 he had saved, Mr. Padron hired one operator and began manufacturing hand-rolled cigars. In 1968, Padron Cigars, Inc., sold more than one million cigars made of tobacco grown with Cuban seeds in Central America.

Mr. Padron's factory is one of some 6,000 Cuban-owned business that in recent years have sprung up in greater Miami exemplifying what observers regard as remarkable economic progress attained by 200,000 exiles living here.

Although many of these businesses are concentrated along 25 blocks of Miami's Southwest 8th Street, called Little Havanna and one of the town's liveliest sections, there is practically no major street in this metropolitan area of 1.3 million without a Cuban-owned garage, grocery, beauty parlor or restaurant.

Mostly Self-Financed

Catering mainly to refugees, but steadily expanding service to the entire community and tourists, Cuban businesses have been by-and-large self-financed.

"I didn't even bother to go to the bank because I knew they could hardly consider giving a loan to an unknown refugee," said Eduardo Sardina, who at the end of 1961 with his father-in-law invested $6,000, almost all they had at the time to start a bakery manufacturing Cuban-style crackers.

Last year, the sales of Wajay Bakery, Inc., exceeded $500,000 and its equipment and delivery trucks have all been paid for.

Ironically, the longevity of the Castro government has contributed to the opening of many exile-owned businesses here.

"When we arrived here, I was convinced we would return home pretty soon, so I began saving because I knew over there we would have to start from scratch," Mr. Padron said.

He added that only after he had decided that he would not be able to go back to Cuba in the immediate future he decided to invest his small savings into cigar making.

The business, now worth about $150,000, was successful from the start, Mr. Padron said, adding with pride that he had not needed any loans and has no financial obligations.

At his small air-conditioned plant, 20 experienced Cuban operators hand-roll daily about 4,200 cigars of 10 sizes and types, ranging from 9-inch gigantes, which retail for $2 each, to 5½-inch cazadoses costing 35 cents each.

Mr. Padron says that even though he sells as much as he can now produce he does not want to grow too fast, lest the quality of the cigars suffers.

While saying that the fragrance of the Pinar del Rio leaf cannot be reproduced anywhere, he added that tobacco grown with Cuban seeds in Honduras and Nicaragua is the nearest to it.

"But adequate sorting, blending and maturing of tobacco are as important as the quality of the leaf," he said, confessing that for all his knowledge of tobacco he still does not know how to hand-roll a first-class cigar, for which a skillful operator uses only his hands and a knife.

80 Per Cent in Cuba

About 80 per cent of Padron cigars are consumed by Cubans in Miami.

The rest is shipped to cities such as New York, Chicago and Philadelphia and to a growing number of custom clients.

One of the latter is Mitch Miller, the conductor, who regularly orders 300 gigantes and who praises them as "the best cigars made in this country."

Wajay Bakery also manufactures principally for the consumption of Cubans, who prefer to eat with their meals dry crackers, whose taste resembles sea biscuits, instead of bread.

Sixty per cent of the bakery's products, which also include bread sticks and sweet rolls, is sold in Miami, with New York being the second largest market.

"At the beginning we thought we would go bankrupt," Mr. Sardina said, recalling that neither he nor his father-in-law, former owner of a meat packing house in Havanna, knew anything about the baking business.

"Only after several long months of trial and error did we finally learn how to make good crackers and we have been growing ever since," added the 47-year old Cuban lawyer turned businessman.

Wajay Bakery employs 52 persons, all Cubans, and has a weekly payroll of $4,000. Its basic product is a five-ounce cellophane-wrapped package of crackers that retails in Miami for 25 cents and of which 9,000 are produced daily. . . .

One of the two military heroes of Cuba's war of independence was Gen. Antonio Maceo, a Negro. Gen. Maceo's grandson, Dr. Antonio Maceo, a physician, also resides here.

Dr. Orta, chief medical resident at Miami Veterans Administration Hospital, said he expected his father, also a physician in his native town of San José de las Lajas in Havana Province, to join him here shortly.

Like all Negro exiles interviewed, Dr. Orta stated he had few contacts with United States Negroes outside the hospital. "We are Cubans and we are regarded as such by the Americans, Negroes and whites alike," Dr. Orta said. "On occasions, I might have felt discriminated against, but as a Cuban, not as a Negro."

Manuel Pinillo is an assistant manager of a Cuban-owned garage, the same job he had in Havanna. He makes over $100 a week, and his wife, a factory worker, $65 a week.

"I'm regarded as a Cuban by all my clients," he stressed.

Mr. Pinillo told another story, which, he said, in a way explained why he, his wife and his son left their homeland.

A Cuban official was interrogating a Negro woman who, with her three small children, was applying for a passport to go to the United States.

"Senora," the official said, "don't you know that over there these negritos /young Negroes/ are worth nothing?

"Whoever told you I'm going to Miami to sell them?" the mother replied. "We are leaving so they can get enough to eat." . . .

SOCIAL SCIENTISTS AND THE POLICE
1970

Antagonism between the police and Blacks has been a chronic irritant in Miami's racial equation. During the twenty-year tenure of Chief Walter Headley (1948-1968), the situation was exacerbated. A former cavalryman, Headley was a "hard liner" who did not consider community relations projects part of the Police Department's responsibility. Leadership attitudes changed significantly when Bernard Garmire succeeded Headley. Garmire was not only interested in community relations projects, but he also initiated a federally funded study program aimed at improving police rapport with the Black community. The following article describes this program, the results of which will have applications for many American cities.

Source: New York Times, November 29, 1970, p. 32.

An extraordinary attempt at racial introspection by a law enforcement agency has been undertaken here. Social scientists, at the request of the Miami Police Department, are attempting to find out what it is that engenders fear and hatred of blacks among white policemen and how deep those emotions are.

The study is continuing, but among the initial conclusions of the specialists are these:

A year or two of service in the ghetto inculcates bigotry toward Negroes among white policemen at least partly because some blacks tend to regard the police as their natural enemy. For the same reason, simpling donning a policeman's uniform can lead to bigotry if it does not exist already.

After a few years a policeman may remain a hard-line bigot, "and show the black who's boss if he steps out of line." Or, if the policeman feels initially that race is not an issue in his work, it almost invariably becomes one because in a black neighborhood most of his trouble comes from blacks.

Rapport is surprisingly good between policemen and black children, the middle-aged and the elderly. The severe hostility found by the social scientists was di-

rected principally at teenagers and young adults.
   One of the strongest emotions among white patrolmen in the ghetto is fear. The analogy is made to military combat; some policemen speal of their nightly patrols in black areas as ventures into "Vietnam."

Many Trying to Cooperate

"More policemen are swinging over to the line that we have to work with blacks," said one of the social scientists conducting the study. "It's the party line in the police department, but it hasn't fully sunk in."
   The police hostility--and the ambivalent attitudes toward blacks in some cases--were buttressed by observations of a visitor who accompanied policemen on a recent night patrol in the ghetto. The residents were routinely referred to as "niggers" and the white policemen acted imperiously toward some, mainly the young men. "I just can't bring myself to call them 'mister'," one policeman conceded.
   The policemen's attitudes were not softened by a message on their patrol car radio reporting that six shots had been fired at colleagues patrolling a different ghetto area.
   The contrast in attitudes toward many of the middle-aged and elderly residents, and especially children, was dramatic. Youngsters besieged the car to banter with the patrolmen and look over their equipment.
   One boy was allowed to use the public address system mounted atop the car. "All you kids get off the street," he yelled, his amplified voice booming out of the speaker as the children and the policemen broke up laughing.
   Later the policemen were directed to investigate a complaint that a rowdy group was disturbing the peace. They drove to the address to find a group of children playing peacefully. The man behind the wheel waved at the children and drove on, grumbling, "some people want us to stamp out smiling."

Accent on Positive

The object of the study is to help accent this positive side of the policeman's demeanor toward blacks by analyzing his bigotry, both latent and developed. Initial indications are that when first assigned to the ghetto the white policeman, regardless of his original prejudices, develops a sense of fear and hostility toward blacks that will linger with him for years, perhaps the rest of his career.
   Once dislike and distrust take hold, according to the study, fear results, leading to the type of overreactions by white police toward blacks that have in turn caused avoidable riots.
   The federally funded study seeks to examine the contacts between the police and the ghetto residents, to de-

termine how much the so-called "ghetto-effect" contributes to the psychological stresses and strains on the policemen, and to seek ways to overcome the difficulties to affect a more peaceful community.

No one is promising miracles, but there are a few indications that the short-term efforts to seek better relations between the police and the ghetto dweller may, at least temporarily have cooled a potentially explosive racial situation. In addition, the aims may be significantly aided in the long run by taking what is being learned and applying it to the future selection, training, and deployment of policemen.

The study, which has not always been regarded favorably by the rank and file patrolmen was instigated by Bernard L. Garmire, who is gaining a national reputation as an unusual and able police chief, especially in the field of community relations.

Although he was appointed almost 18 months ago, it was only last summer that Mr. Garmire, after a series of internal power struggles, was able to assert his authority over the department, elevate to higher commands men in his own image, and start a five-year plan of reform to be aided by the studies now going on.

Chief Garmire, formerly police chief in Tucson, Ariz., and Eau Claire, Wis., was chosen for the job after the death of Walter E. Headley, a hard-line police chief of the old school who told his men during the race riots here in 1968:

"There is only one way to handle looters and arsonists during a riot and that is to shoot them on sight. I've let the word filter down: When the looting starts, the shooting starts."

The result was three dead and a score wounded. In contrast, during the disturbances here in June half a dozen persons were wounded, none killed. Because of the different nature of the two sets of riots it is impossible to state with authority that the softer tactics paid off in saving lives and injuries, but the police say it has helped.

"I think we can accomplish much more by using honey rather than vinegar. But I do believe in being prepared to use vinegar," said Chief Garmire whose soft-spoken, urbane manner belies his 33 years of police work.

"We have some bigots and some who want to take the hard line, there is no question of that," he went on. "But we're trying to eliminate the hiring of bigots and I think we're making some progress."

The idea of approaching the Federal Government for funds to study the department originated, Chief Garmire said, "after there were several shootouts here, and every time there was a confrontation it was apparent that there was more stress and strain on the officers." . . .

BIBLIOGRAPHY

The following bibliography is designed to suggest interesting and profitable directions to researchers or leisure readers. No exhaustive listing of unpublished sources, newspapers and primary materials has been attempted. The criteria for selection have been relevance, quality, variety, and accessibility. Occasionally, one or more of these criteria have been violated to permit the inclusion of particularly important or interesting works. The brief listing of "Official Publications" is intended to indicate the variety of materials that is available. There is no adequate single-volume history of Miami, and it is especially difficult to find informative literature on the 1930-1955 period. Nonetheless, a reasonable introduction to the subject can be gleaned from a combination of the Federal Writers' Project's <u>Miami and Dade County</u>, Isidor Cohen's <u>Historical Sketches</u>, Frank B. Sessa's "Real Estate Expansion and Boom in Miami," and Edward Sofen's <u>The Miami Metropolitan Experiment</u>. <u>Tequesta</u> and the <u>Florida Historical Quarterly</u> provide the richest periodical sources, and the <u>Miami Herald</u> is the most informative newspaper.

PRIMARY SOURCES

Official Publications

Dade County, Florida, County Manager. <u>Six Year Capital Improvements Program, 1962-1968</u>. Miami, 1962.

Dade County, Florida, Development Department. <u>Economic Survey of Metropolitan Miami</u>. Miami, 1959.

Dade County, Florida, Government Research Council. <u>Local Government in Dade County</u>. Miami, 1965.

strong on the 1895-1900 period and includes an appendix on the attempted assassination of Franklin D. Roosevelt in 1933.

Weigall, Theyre H. *Boom in Paradise*. New York, 1932. An incisive and often humorous account of Miami's boom years by an English journalist who participated fully.

SECONDARY SOURCES

Books

American National Red Cross. *The Florida Hurricane, September 18, 1926.* Washington, D.C., 1927. An account of Miami's most devastating storm and the subsequent recovery operation.

Ballinger, Kenneth. *Miami Millions: The Dance of the Dollars in the Great Florida Land Boom of 1925.* Miami, 1936. An entertaining piece by someone who knew Miami and, at least superficially, Miamians; plenty of anecdotes.

Barbour, Ralph H. *Let's Go Florida!* New York, 1926

Beach, Rex Ellingwood. *The Miracle of Coral Gables.* New York, 1926.

Brinton, Daniel G. *Notes on the Floridian Peninsula, Its Literary History, Indian Tribes and Antiquities*, Philadelphia, 1859. Brinton, an archaeologist, provides valuable information on Florida's Indians and explorers.

Canova, Andrew P. *Life and Adventures in South Florida*. Palatka, Florida, 1885.

Carson, Ruby and Charlton W. Tebeau. *Florida: From Indian Trail to Space Age*. 3 vols. Delray Beach, Florida, 1966. A valuable source by highly qualified historians.

Chamberlain, John Newton. *Miami, Jewel of the South*. /Miami?/, 1921.

DeCrois, F. W. *Historical, Industrial and Commercial Data of Miami and Fort Lauderdale, Dade County*, Florida. St. Augustine, Florida, 1909.

Federal Writers' Project, Florida. *Florida: A Guide to the Southernmost State*. New York, 1939. Contains a

BIBLIOGRAPHY

Dade County, Florida, Planning Department. <u>Magic City Center: Economic Appraisal and Projections</u>. Miami, 1960.

Miami Chamber of Commerce, Miami, Florida, Industrial Department. <u>The City of Miami: Industrial Survey</u>. Miami, 1938.

Miami, Publicity Department. <u>City of Miami, Florida, Golden Anniversary, 1896-1946, Fifty Years of Progress</u>. Miami, 1946.

Miami-Dade County Chamber of Commerce, Government Research Council. <u>Metropolitan Dade County: What It Is; What It Has Done; What It Can Do; What Is Its Effect on the Costs of Government</u>. Miami, 1961.

United State National Commission on the Causes and Prevention of Violence, Miami Study Team. <u>Miami Report</u>. Miami, 1969. A particularly well done piece on the August 1968 violence in Miami.

Memoirs and Accounts by Contemporaries

Blackman, E. V. <u>Miami and Dade County, Florida: Its Settlement, Progress and Achievement</u>. Washington, D.C., 1921. An interesting account of all facets of early Miami life combined with series of biographical sketches on Miami pioneers.

Cohen, Isidor. <u>Historical Sketches and Sidelights of Miami, Florida.</u> Miami, 1925. A delightful book from an early Miamian with a fine sense of humor.

Dorn, J. K. "Recollections of Early Miami /1870-1898/," <u>Tequesta</u>, 9 (1949), 43-59. A valuable source of material from an early resident, but marred by lack of dates.

Escalante, Fontaneda, Hernando d'. <u>Memoir of D^o d'Escalante Fontaneda Respecting Florida</u>, trans. from the Spanish with notes by Buckingham Smith, reprinted with revisions. Miami, 1944. A brief account by a Spaniard marooned in Southeast Florida in the 16th century.

Rainbolt, Victor. <u>The Town That Climate Built</u>. Miami, 1926. An account of Miami between 1896 and the mid-1920's written in semi-memoir style.

Sewell, John. <u>John Sewell's Memoirs and History of Miami, Florida</u>. Miami, 1933. Written by an early citizen and mayor of Miami, this account is particularly fourteen page section on Miami which is of limited use.

--------. *Miami and Dade County* (American Guide Series). Northport, N.Y., 1941. A useful source which provides some bibliographic help as well.

--------. *The Seminole Indians in Florida*. Talahassee, Florida, 1940.

--------. *The Spanish Missions of Florida*. St. Augustine, Florida, 1940.

Fagen, Richard R., et. al. *Cubans in Exile: Disaffection and the Revolution*. Stanford, 1967. This book analyzes who the exiles are and why they left Cuba; based primarily on questionnaires administered to Cuban refugees in Miami (1958-1962).

Fisher, Jane. *The Fabulous Hoosier*. New York, 1947. The subject of this volume is Carl Graham Fisher; the author was his first wife whom he divorced in 1926.

Fox, Charles D. *The Truth About Florida*. New York, 1925. A typical piece of literature provoked by Florida's and Miami's great land boom.

Glendening, Parris N. "The Metropolitan Dade County Government: An Examination of Reform," Ph. D. dissertation, Florida State University, 1967. A useful reference dealing with the background, implementation and effect of Miami-Dade County's Metro government.

Redford, Polly. *Billion Dollar Sandbar: A Biography of of Miami Beach*. New York, 1970.

Roberts, Kenneth L. *Florida*. New York and London, 1926. While this book deals with Florida rather than specifically with Miami, it is informative on the land boom phenomenon; a condescending tone dominates the analysis.

Serino, Gustave. Miami's Metropolitan Experiment (Civic Information Series No. 28). Gainesville, Florida, 1958.

Sessa, Frank B. "Real Estate Expansion and Boom in Miami and its Environs During the 1920's, " Ph.D. Dissertation, University of Pittsburgh, 1950. A detailed treatment of the 1923-1926 period, it is a valuable study which highlights the positive as well as the negative aspects of the boom.

Sofen, Edward. The Miami Metropolitan Experiment (Metropolitan Action Studies No. 2). Bloomington, Indiana, 1963. A particularly fine work. Sofen traces the roots of Metro back to 1943, analyzes its creation, and comments on its implementation, problems and potential as of 1962.

--------. A Report on Politics in Greater Miami. Cambridge, Massachusetts, 1961.

Tebeau, Charlton W. A History of Florida. Coral Gables, Florida, 1971. A well-executed study by a prominent historian; the narrative is heavily political but contains sufficient social and economic material for balance.

Wolff, Reinhold P. Miami, Economic Pattern of a Resort Area. Coral Gables, Florida, 1945. A study designed to promote long-range economic planning in Miami and South Florida.

Articles

"An 1870 Itinerary from St. Augustine to Miami," Florida Historical Quarterly (hereinafter cited FHQ), 18 (1940), 204-215.

Adams, Adam G. "Some Pre-boom Developers of Dade County," Tequesta, 17 (1957), 31-46.

Barron, Clarence W. "Winter Wall Street; Diagnosis of Florida Land Speculations," Barron's; the National Financial Weekly, VII, No. 18 (May 2, 1927), 8. This is an example of the kind of article which appeared in many financial journals across the nation during and after the Florida land boom. Other examples appear below and can be identified by title and date.

Bartlett, Willard A. "Opportunities and Dangers in Florida," Barron's; the National Financial Weekly, VI, No. 7 (Feb. 8, 1926), 10. A fairly balanced view of the land boom written with an anti-Spanish bias.

Bingham, Millicent Todd. "Miami: A Study in Urban Geography," Tequesta, 8 (1948), 73-107.

Boone, John and Wm. Farmer. "Violence in Miami; One More Warning," New South, 23 (Fall 1968), 28-37. This article deals with the August 1968 uprisings in Miami.

Buchanan, Patricia. "Miami's Bootleg Boom," Tequesta,

30 (1970), 13-31.

Burt, A. "Miami: The Cuban Flavor," Nation, 212 (March 8, 1971), 299-302. Burt, an editorial writer for the Miami Herald, provides a good article on the contributions made by Cubans to Miami and some of the problems created by them.

Carney, James J. "Population Growth in Miami and Dade County, Florida," Tequesta, 6 (1946), 50-55.

Carson, Ruby Leach. "Miami: 1896-1900," Tequesta, 16 (1956), 3-13. An informative piece apparently drawn heavily from the memoirs of Sewell and Cohen and from the Metropolis, an early Miami newspsper.

--------. "Forty Years of Miami Beach," Tequesta, 15 (1955), 3-27.

Chamberlain, Lucy J. "Behind the Boom in Florida," Survey, LV (Feb. 1, 1925), 529-533.

Claussen, Dean R. "Metro Government and the Cities of Dade County," Florida Municipal Record, 32 (July 1958), 21.

Corliss, Carlton J. "Henry M. Flagler--Railroad Builder," FHQ, 38 (1960), 195-205. The subject of this article was the Standard Oil partner-railroad builder who contributed greatly to Miami's early development.

Einstein, Paul. "Urban Renewal and Metro Dade," American County Government, 31 (June 1966), 15-17.

Essary, Jesse F. "Have Faith in Florida," New Republic, XLIV (Oct. 14, 1925), 194-196. This article describes the speculation of the period but does not warn of impending doom as many commentators at that time did.

Fagen, Richard R. and Richard A. Brody. "Cubans in Exile, a Demographic Analysis," Social Problems, 11 (Spring 1964), 389-401. This article is based on data collected in the Miami area.

Gearhart, Ernest G., Jr. "South Florida's First Industry," Tequesta, 12 (1952), 55-57. The author describes the arrowroot starch industry of Dade County.

"Growth Trends in Greater Miami," Economic Research, (Jan. 1955), 1-2. The author discusses major economic developments in 1954.

BIBLIOGRAPHY

Head, J.M. "Chasing the Rainbow in Florida," *Magazine of Wall Street*, XXXVII (Nov. 21, 1925), 106-109.

Hudson, F.M. "Beginnings in Dade County," *Tequesta*, 3 (1943), 1-35.

"Jet Stream to Vietnam via Miami," *Business Week*, (Jan. 14, 1967), 112-114. An interesting piece on five companies near Miami's International Airport that overhauled warplanes engaged in Vietnam combat.

Kowalsky, Stanley. "What has Metro Accomplished for Dade?," *The Miamian* [Miami-Dade Chamber of Commerce], September 1966, entire issue.

Lardner, G., Jr. "Epidemic of Law and Order; W. Headley's War on Negro Offenders," *Nation*, 206 (Feb. 19, 1968), 231-234. Lardner, then a *Washington Post* reporter, presents a critical discussion of Police Chief Headley's 1967-1968 "War on Crime"; a good piece for the liberal viewpoint.

Laumer, Frank J. "The Fort Dade Site," *Florida Anthropology*, 16 (1963), 33-42.

McCullagh, Francis. "Miami; Florida Boom," *Nineteenth Century*, XCIX (Feb. 1926), 211-212.

"Meat Riot; Brownsville," *Newsweek*, 75 (June 29, 1970), 20-21.

Metzger, Joseph P. "Metro and Its Judicial History," *University of Miami Law Review*, 15 (1961), 283-292. This report covers a fascinating facet of Metro's development.

"Miami Captures a Fleet: New Seaport," *Business Week*, (Jan. 18, 1969), 24-25. A useful description of Miami's increasing cruise business.

"Miami in 1843," *FHQ*, 3 (1925), 34-35. A piece excerpted from *The News* (St. Augustine, Florida) of December 30, 1843.

Morrison, A. "Miami's Cuban Refugee Crisis," *Ebony*, 18 (June 1963), 96-100+. A good article that explores the problems that the first wave of Cuban refugees created for Miami's Black citizens.

Nevin, D. "Mr. Million Miami Missed," *Life*, 53 (Aug. 17, 1962), 13. A description of Miami's humorous experience with its millionth citizen.

Permutter, Nathan. "Bombing in Miami," Commentary, 25 (June 1958), 498-503. A good piece by the then Director of the Florida Office of the Anti-Defamation League. It discusses the connection made by some Southern white extremists between anti-Semitism and segregation.

Rose, Harold M. "Metropolitan Miami's Changing Negro Population, 1950-1960," Economic Geography, 40 (July 1964), 221-238.

Rubinstein, Marion. "Construction is the Key to Miami's Current Boom," Municipal South, 14 (Jan. 1967), 7-13.

Ryan, William T. "Miami: The Non-city," Business and Economic Dimensions, 3 (July 1967), 15-18. This article discusses the city's historical development and its growth prospects, particularly in relation to the downtown area.

Samet, Elaine R. "Quiet Revolution in Miami," Progressive, 29 (April 1965), 34-37. A discussion of the peaceful (to 1965 at least) nature of Miami's civil rights activities.

Schellings, William J. "Soldiers in Miami, 1898," Tequesta, 17 (1957), 69-76.

Sessa, Frank B. "Anti-Florida Propaganda and Counter Measures During the 1920's," Tequesta, 21 (1961), 41-51.
--------. "Miami in 1926," Tequesta, 16 (1956), 15-36.

Shappee, Nathan D. "Zangara's Attempted Assassination of Franklin D. Roosevelt," FHQ, 37 (1958), 101-110.

Sofen, Edward. "Financial Dilemma Miami-Dade Style," National Civic Review, 51 (April 1962), 220-222.

--------. "Problems of Metropolitan Leadership: The Miami Experience," Midwest Journal of Political Science, V (Feb. 1961), 18-38.

Sofge, Haley. "Public Housing in Miami," Florida Planning and Development, 19 (Mar. 1968), 1-4.

Thayer, Yvonne. "Havana, Florida: Cubans Thrive in Miami Area," Wall Street Journal, (Dec. 11, 1969), 1+. This article contains informative comments on the economic success of Cubans in Miami.

Tornillo, Pat L., Jr. "In Dade Co., Florida," NEA Journal, 52 (Dec. 1963), 51-52. An article by a Dade

County teacher which discusses how the Black and white teachers of Miami-Dade joined in one organization.

Walsh, B. O. "Cubans in Miami," *America*, 114 (Feb. 26, 1966), 286-289.

Wilmott, John F. "The Truth About City-County Consolidation," *Miami Law Quarterly*, II (Dec. 1947), 127-179. A pre-Metro discussion of Miami-Dade County cooperation and consolidation efforts.

Wilson, F. Page. "Miami: From Frontier to Metropolis; An Appraisal," *Tequesta*, 14 (1954), 25-49.

Wolff, Reinhold P. "Recent Economic Trends in South Florida," Tequesta, 4 (1944), 45-49.

Wood, Thomas J. "Dade County: Unbossed, Erratically Led," *The Annals of the American Academy of Political and Social Science*, 353 (May 1964), 64-71.

NAME INDEX

Alderman, Horace, 26
Alexander, Donald C., 64
Amod, E., 28
Anderson, Robert H., 51
Aptheker, Herbert, 57
Armour, Philip, 6
Aronovitz, Abraham, 44, 45
Ashe, Bowman F., 21
Astor, Vincent, 6

Barton, Fred W., 16, 40
Beasley, Edmund D., 3
Bell, Margaret Hawkesworth, 30
Blackman, E. V., 7
Boyles, S., 62
Brickell, Edith, 10
Brickell, William, 3, 4
Brooks, H., 15
Brossier, C. D., 12
Brown, William Mack, 5
Bryan, William Jennings, 19
Buchanan, J. C., 52

Carter, Aaron, 2
Carey, Max, 24
Cermak, Anton J., 29
Campbell, O. W., 47, 51, 52, 53
Cannon, Pat, 49
Capone, Al, 27
Castro, Fidel, 52, 56
Chase, Henry, 9
Chekika, 2
Chiari, Roberto Francisco, 55
Christmas, Randall N., 45
Churchill, Winston S., 38
Clark, William, 57, 58

Coe, C. S., 16
Collins, John S., 12
Crandon, Charles H., 55
Curtiss, Glenn, 12, 14

Danner, Richard G., 41
Darrow, Clarence, 17
Davis, Darrey A., 48
Dean, S. Bobo, 9
Deering, James, 14
Dewey, J. R., 7
Douglas, Marjory Stoneman, 14
DuBose, John, 32, 33
Dupont, Alfred I., 28
Dupont, T. Coleman, 17

Earhart, Amelia, 31
Eaton, J., 62
Egan, John, 1
Eisenhower, Dwight D., 43, 46
English, William F., 2, 3
d'Escalante Fontaneda, Hernando, 1
Evans, E. E., 49, 50

Fair, T. Willard, 61
Farrar, Geradine, 17
Ferguson, George, 2
Ferguson, Ralph B., 32, 33
Ferguson, Thomas, 2
Ferre, Maurice A., 58, 62, 63
Firestone, Harvey S., 17
Fisher, Carl G., 12, 13, 15
Fisher, Charles M., 17, 32
Flagler, Henry M., 4-8, 10, 12, 13
Floyd, Robert C., 40, 41

Forster, S. K., 4
Fossey, A. D. H., 29, 30
Friend, A. B., 11

Garmire, Bernard L., 59, 61
Gautier, Redmond B., 27
Gill, Howard, 11
Gorden, John B., 18

Hall, R. E., 9, 17
Hanna, Mark, 6
Hardie, Dan, 11
Harding, Warren G., 6, 17
Headley, Walter, 41, 43, 52, 58, 59
Heifetz, Jascha, 17
Henderson, Parker A., 13
Herin, William A., 48
Hermance, A. H., 26
High, Robert King, 48, 49, 50, 52, 53, 54, 56, 57

Ingraham, James E., 4

Jackson, James M., 21
Jaudon, J. F., 13
Jeans, Paul G., 30
Kennedy, David, 61, 62
Kennedy, John F., 53
King, Martin Luther, 57
Knight, J. S., 32
Knowlton, A. C., 5

Lewis, Frank, 1
Liddy, W. J., 15
Loeffler, Charles D., 16
Lummus, J. E., 8

McFarlane, Flora, 4
McLeod, John, 53, 54
McNayr, Irving C., 53, 55
Manning, Warren H., 21

Menendez de Aviles, Pedro, 1
Merrick, George E., 16, 17, 18
Merritt, Z. T., 9
Middleton, Ralph, 4
Mill, William F., 13
Moore, Harry T., 43
Moore, T. V., 10

Nation, Carrie, 11

Orr, Alexander, Jr., 34

Pallot, William L., 49
Palmer, Perrine, Jr., 38
Peacock, Jack, 4
Pearson, Ray H., 50
Penny, J. C., 17
Perrine, Henry, 2
Perry, A. H., 14
Picola, James, 51
Ponce de Leon, Juan, 1
Pryor, Arthur, 17

Rachmaninoff, Sergei, 17
Range, Athalie, 61
Reboso, M., 62
Reeder, C. H., 28
Reese, Melvin L., 52, 54, 59
Reilly, John, 6
Rockefeller, John D., 6
Romfh, Edward C., 11, 18, 20, 25
Roosevelt, Franklin D., 29

Schumann-Heink, Ernestine, 17
Senerchia, Chelsie J., 43
Sewell, E. G., 5, 27, 29, 33, 34
Sewell, John, 5, 9
Sibley, Marion E., 46, 47

Smith, Rodman B., 11, 12
Smith, W. P., 15
Spanish Marie, 26
Stoneman, Frank B., 11
Sturtevant, E. T., 3
Sullivan, Jimmy, 42

Thompson, Leonard K., 37
Toulmin, Harry T., 51
Traymor, Pie, 24
Tuttle, Julia, 1, 3, 4, 5, 6, 7

Virrick, Elizabeth, 41

Watson, John W., 12, 14
Watt, Paul C., 50
Wever, Laurie L., 21
Wharton, Frank H., 10, 18
Williams, Robert B., 31, 32, 33
Willard, Ira F., 50, 52
Wilse, James T., 32
Wolforth, William M., 41